WHEN THE GAME STANDS TALL

MOVIE DEVOTIONAL

Foreword by
DAN BRITTON
Executive Vice President for the Fellowship of Christian Athletes

Devotions by
NEIL WILSON

BASED ON THE MOTION PICTURE "WHEN THE GAME STANDS TALL"

Motion Picture based on the Book by
NEIL HAYES

Story by
SCOTT MARSHALL SMITH and DAVID ZELON

Screenplay by
SCOTT MARSHALL SMITH

BroadStreet

BroadStreet Publishing™
Racine, WI 53403
Broadstreetpublishing.com

When The Game Stands Tall Movie Devotional

ISBN 978-1-4245-4907-8

Produced with the assistance of Livingstone, the publishing services division of
the Barton-Veerman Company (www.livingstonecorp.com). Devotions written by
Neil Wilson. Project staff includes Neil Wilson, Dave Veerman, and Linda Taylor.

All film characters and film quotes are from the motion picture *WHEN THE
GAME STANDS TALL*.

Designed by Chris Garborg | garborgdesign.com

Printed in the United States of America.

We are all certain to face some adversity in our lives: some harder to overcome than others. Having a man of remarkable faith and character stand beside you, coach you, mentor you, and lead by example is a treasure almost too difficult to describe. Coach Lad is that man. He taught us that even the smallest details in our lives and how we act or react have consequences. And, that working diligently and leaning on your faith when times get tough can get you through anything. That is what being a De La Salle Spartan is all about. Les Hommes De Foi! We are men of faith!

—FORMER SPARTAN, CAMERON COLVIN
CEO, CamColvin Inc.

INTRODUCTION

When The Game Stands Tall movie is inspired by a remarkable true story about a coach and a football team, featuring exciting action, big hits, and game-changing plays. More than workouts, practices, and Friday night lights, the film features individual and team struggles and triumphs, victories and defeats, relationships and dreams. It is filled with life lessons for Coach Ladouceur (Coach Lad) and the other coaches, for the young athletes, for the parents and other fans of the team... and for us. This book was written to give you the opportunity to think through those faith-and-life lessons and apply them to your own experience.

Each of the 52 devotionals highlights a biblical truth that is illustrated in the movie *When The Game Stands Tall*. Topics begin with a quote from Scripture and sometimes one from the film, and move directly into a real-life application of the biblical truth. This is followed by a challenge for personal reflection and an opportunity to write thoughts and feelings in the space provided.

Read. Apply. Respond.

FOREWORD

"In all the work you are doing, work the best you can. Work as if you were doing it for the Lord, not for people" (Colossians 3:23, NCV).

Coach Lad understands how to capture the hearts of his players. In the movie, *When The Game Stands Tall*, he emphasizes that he isn't looking for perfect performance; rather, perfect effort. He only asks his teams to control what they can control. Performance is not completely controllable, but effort is. As a result, his players strive to be the best they can be by giving their very best.

I am reminded of the story of five-time All-Pro Green Bay Packers lineman Jerry Kramer (1958-1968). Legendary Coach Vince Lombardi rode him really hard in the 1959 preseason. Jerry wanted to quit until one day Coach Lombardi told Jerry that he could become the greatest lineman in the NFL. That one encounter transformed Jerry. He decided to give 100% to every play in practice and games and became one of the greatest players because he understood and applied the concept of perfect effort.

In Colossians 3:23, Paul defines perfect effort. He encourages us to give our best in everything *for God*, not for people. Perfect effort, therefore, applies to every dimension of our lives: mental, physical, emotional, social, and spiritual. When it comes to spiritual effort, I live by one key principle: *we do the training, but God does the changing*. I control my part, and God does the rest. The key is to strive and stretch ourselves in every area to reach our God-given potential. Paul wrote in 1 Corinthians 9:24 that only one runner wins a race, but they all run to win. How are you running?

I am excited that you have decided to read this powerful devotional. You will learn how to become spiritually fit in ways you never imagined. This book is a great blend of reading and reflecting, helping prepare you to become strong and develop a solid spiritual foundation for your life. Preparation always creates fertile ground for change. Often we rush into life without much intentional preparation time, but it can be the most rewarding and revealing part of the journey.

This is a great playbook to prepare you for the game of life. If you want to be a difference maker, start today and begin your training so God can start the changing. You can't control the outcome, but you can control the effort.

Take time, dig deep, and enjoy the journey.

—DAN BRITTON

Executive Vice President of International Ministry and Training, Fellowship of Christian Athletes and co-author of *One Word That Will Change Your Life*, *WisdomWalks*, and *WisdomWalks SPORTS*.

WHEN DOES THE GAME STAND TALL?

I'm not saying I'm the best coach. I'm just saying I've seen a lot of teams. I think that's my strength as a coach. I'm not a genius. I'm not brilliant as a coach. But my strength is being able to tell you guys if you are playing up to your abilities.

—COACH LAD
From the movie *WHEN THE GAME STANDS TALL*

Don't you realize that in a race everyone runs, but only one person gets the prize? So run to win!
(1 Corinthians 9:24, NLT)

American English is always on the move. The word *game* isn't just a noun describing an athletic event or an interesting diversion with cards or a board. Now the word is often used as a synonym for ability, as in the question, "Have you got game?" Coach Lad is known for his expectation—not that his players will produce perfection, but that they will commit to a perfect effort. The game *stands tall* when those playing the game rise above their abilities and appreciate the larger life that surrounds the field and can be changed by the game.

Throughout the movie, *When The Game Stands Tall*, the point is made in many ways that what's most important isn't the game itself but the people in the game and what the game brings out of them.

For Coach Lad, the game of football is a setting where he can help young men discover who they are at their best. The history of the De LaSalle teams is marked by outstanding athletes who excelled at higher levels of the sport, but the teams also featured many regular players who contributed in ways not often noticed by the stat-keepers and the evaluators of talent.

The Apostle Paul didn't just believe in participation in the life of faith. He encouraged those who entered the race to run to win. At the very least, he wanted followers of Jesus to run to finish. When he wrote what could have been his epitaph, he said, "I have fought the good fight, I have finished the race, I have kept the faith" (2 Timothy 4:7, NKJV). He wanted to finish strong. Only one wins the race, but each person runs as well as he or she can—or not. Running to win doesn't always mean winning; it does mean fighting well and finishing the challenge.

Paul was doing what the graduating seniors on Coach Lad's teams often do—acknowledging the end of their time and encouraging those coming behind them to make the most of their opportunity. Paul wanted young Timothy to do well, even as the end of his own time approached.

In the closing game of the film, with the team championship secured and Chris's individual rushing achievement in sight, the players, led by Chris, chose to honor the coach by demonstrating the deeper lessons learned from him. They wanted to show Coach Lad they understood that more than a football game was at stake and that what they meant to each other was more than the score or the record. Yes, they played to win, but they also played for one another and their coach in ways that mattered more than the game.

That choice made their game stand tall.

....

....

....

....

....

....

....

....

....

....

....

....

....

....

....

....

....

WHAT MAKES A SPARTAN?

Commitment. Accountability. Perfect effort. And finally love. This bond is what has led countless Spartans to achieve far more than anyone, including themselves, believed they were capable of. Without it, you may continue to win football games but you will have lost the chance to become Spartans.

—COACH LAD
From the movie *WHEN THE GAME STANDS TALL*

Therefore I, a prisoner for serving the Lord, beg you to lead a life worthy of your calling, for you have been called by God. Always be humble and gentle. Be patient with each other, making allowance for each other's faults because of your love (Ephesians 4:1–2, NLT).

Although we live in a highly individualistic society, the truth remains that the best things in life involve other people. Notice Coach Lad's four characteristics of Spartans: commitment, accountability, perfect effort, and love. How many of those can you do alone, and how many require at least one other person? Commitment is something we make, but we make it to a team or a person. Accountability requires a mutual agreement between people to be held to certain standards. Perfect effort takes on deeper meaning when combined with the efforts of others. And the glue is love.

People with a high level of ability, represented by Tayshon in the movie, can easily think they don't need the teamwork aspects of the game—like practice and drills. Athleticism can lead to narcissism, where a person downplays the role of the rest of the team because he is solely focused on his own contribution. This is the opposite of love, which looks out for others not just one's self. Every position on the football field relies on the other ten teammates.

When the Apostle Paul wrote to the Ephesians, he spent the first half of the letter coaching Christians about the basics of the faith and how being "in Christ" makes all the difference. But in chapter 4, he switches gears into almost a locker-room speech. In essence, he is saying, "I've been teaching and training you. The time has come to get in the game and put our drills and training into practice. You've been preparing to be a team; now it's time to act like a team." Paul mentions five qualities—humility, gentleness, patience, putting up with each other, and love—as the necessary components of an active faith. Like Coach Lad, he makes love the central part of teamwork.

Notice that love makes allowance for others' faults. Athletes on losing teams spend time highlighting the mistakes and poor plays of teammates. Instead of being a unified group that works together to achieve a goal, a team like that becomes merely a collection of individuals often going in different directions. Nothing destroys a team quicker than pointing out the failures of others. In contrast, love means encouraging teammates and affirming them for what they do right.

This biblical principle applies beyond the football field. Successful families pull together—with love. The same is true for churches, businesses, clubs, music groups, and more. Love makes all the difference.

What can you do to be a more loving person?

WATCHFUL

Watch, stand fast in the faith, be brave, be strong
(1 Corinthians 16:13, NKJV).

This verse is a particular challenge from the Apostle Paul for men. It's not age specific, so no matter how old you are, the verse applies to you as a man. This time we will only look at the word *watch*. In the ancient Greek, it's actually a military term for watchfulness and being on guard. It's all about paying attention.

Football players watching themselves on film takes some getting used to. What they thought was a nice fluid motion on the field is often captured on camera as though they were barely keeping from tripping over their own feet. But once the embarrassing phase is over, looking at game films is an amazing tool for working on technique and for studying their own and the other team's tendencies. The camera captures a lot. Someone who knows how to analyze film can help the players get a lot out of what they are watching.

A problem with watching film is that you can't watch the game. Instead, you are looking at a small game within the larger game, and you have to decide what exactly you are going to keep your eye on. If you are a linebacker, you may want to watch every third down play your opponent ran in an entire game. Do you find tendencies that show up when you focus on those particular plays? Or what about a wide receiver who will be your assignment during the game? How does he set up his cuts to the left or the right? What's his stronger turn? Do you see other tendencies? Does he come back for the ball, or does he give up on the play if the pass is short?

The more you watch film attentively, the more you develop what is called in the military "situational awareness." You develop a sense of what might happen even though you may not be able to describe *how* you know. Your brain simply picks up signals it has seen before and sees a pattern you can react to. Players sometimes describe it as watching the game slow down so they see things unfold and can react as they should, even though in real time things are happening very quickly.

In the larger scheme of things, we often let life happen around us without really paying a lot of attention. Who are the ten most important people in your life? Do they know that? What was the last thing you did for each of them that allowed them to sense you appreciated them? When we think about approaching all of life in a more watchful way, the people who matter ought to be at the top of our list of what not to miss. If you can sense how much it means to you when someone notices and appreciates you, you can imagine doing the same thing for them. After all, as Jesus said, we need to treat others as we want to be treated.

Who is at the top of your list of what not to miss?

....

....

....

....

....

....

....

....

....

....

....

....

....

....

....

....

....

....

LES HOMMES DE FOI

Be on guard. Stand firm in the faith. Be courageous.
Be strong (1 Corinthians 16:13, NLT).

Les Hommes De Foi is the motto of De LaSalle High School. The French expression translates into English as *Men of Faith*. As a Roman Catholic affiliated school run by the Christian Brothers, training in the Christian faith is part of the curriculum and is the underlying expectation for life on campus. The school website makes it clear that the school will represent a "living expression of the Good News" and will be an atmosphere for "dialogue in truth, freedom, and hope." These are helpful ways of understanding what's expected of men of faith.

When the Apostle Paul was challenging the believers in Corinth, he included in his short list his expectation that they would "stand firm in the faith." The *standing firm* part of his expression was a military word in Greek that meant holding ground and taking a stand. The picture fits that decisive moment that happens in every play in football when either the defensive or the offensive line succeeds in moving the opposing players in a certain direction. Other expressions, like "maintaining the pocket," "driving the line back," or "gap control" all point to a certain part of standing firm. Standing firm involves knowing where you're going on the field or what space you're going to hold and holding it. Holding a block is standing firm.

All these aspects of football illustrate what Paul had in mind as a character trait for disciples of Jesus. But we should note that it wasn't just standing firm in any old place. It wasn't about having a certain view and being stubborn. His point was that authentic followers of Jesus Christ are not moved from their faith.

Unfortunately, the word *faith* has become highly personalized today—as if people get to make up their own ideas of God and create a set of beliefs for themselves. This is a very popular idea, but it's not Christianity. The faith referenced by Paul is the faith described in the Bible and the creeds of the church. Part of standing firm means holding true to what Christians have always believed and not being moved or shifted by the current trends. The big problem with *current* and *trends* is that nothing is firm about them. Currents and trends drift like the ocean and can't support the weight that instead we can rest on the "faith once delivered to the saints."

Part of the reason we read and think about the Bible, learn the creeds, and undergo training within the church is to develop our understanding of the faith so we can stand firm in it and on it. Knowing what we believe is important. Belief doesn't just float by itself; it must be rooted in a set of statements we believe to be profoundly true and by which we order our lives. If you don't know what you believe, you can't very well stand firm in it.

What should you do to learn more about the faith?

ACT LIKE MEN

Be watchful, stand firm in the faith, act like men,
be strong (1 Corinthians 16:13, ESV).

For many young men and women, athletic achievement is a rite of passage that introduces them to adult responsibility and maturity. Teamwork, in particular, forces them to think beyond their own interests or desires and pursue what will benefit the entire team. On many high school teams, the underclassmen look at seniors as the role models for behavior and attitude as they prepare for their time as the advanced group.

Throughout the film, *When The Game Stands Tall*, we see a strong sense of a set of expectations that goes with the title of Spartan. And alumni don't hesitate to call out current players with the challenge to act like Spartans. Coach Lad makes the point in at least one speech that being a Spartan is a lot more than wearing the jersey. T.K. confronts Chris and Danny in the diner with the reality that they will have to step up and lead as they haven't before. They have been given positions on the team; now it's time to step up.

Acting like a man certainly has its solo moments, such as when you have to make a hard choice to care for someone. In the example above, T.K. has moved past the finish line for his high school career and is moving on, but he makes the individual choice to extend a hand to guys coming after him with some encouragement and truth. Acting like a man is also understanding the role of others in our lives and not trying to do everything alone. Acting like a man is not solitary toughness but working out what it means to fully do your part in solidarity with others. The clashes between Tayshon's character and Chris and Danny in the film revolve around their efforts to draw him into full participation in the team. Tayshon thinks that being a man means not caring for the rest of the team and standing on his own talent, while the two leaders continually try to pull him into the more important task of being part of something bigger and more significant—what they are all becoming *together*.

Acting like a man also means recognizing we were made and put on this earth by a God who loves us and designed us a certain way. We act like men when we are praying the Lord's Prayer, "Your kingdom come, your will be done, on earth as it is in heaven," and we make that request personal: "Lord, let your way of doing things and your will about things be as real in my life as it is in heaven." Jesus was acting like a man when He said to His Father, "Your will be done." He had just prayed basically, "If there's any way this cup of suffering on the cross could pass from me, I'd be all for that, Father," even though He already knew that wouldn't be the case. He did what needed to be done. We follow His example in acting like men when we face those things we don't really want to do but know must be done, and we do them.

In what ways do you need to act more like a man?

....

....

....

....

....

....

....

....

....

....

....

....

....

....

....

....

....

....

STRENGTH TRAINING

Be on the alert, stand firm in the faith, act like men,
be strong (1 Corinthians 16:13, NASB).

Paul's fourth guideline for Christian men is found in the phrase "be strong." What could be more manly than being strong? Men may not always be sensitive or thoughtful, but we don't want to be accused of not being strong. Give us something to lift, push, or throw. When we take on a challenge, we don't want to put out a weak effort.

The modern age of sports has emphasized strength training unheard of in previous generations. Stronger athletes can do the mechanics and the techniques of their sport longer and better than gifted athletes who are weak physically. This understanding of the importance of strength has unfortunately led, in some cases, to athletes trying to artificially pump themselves up in ways that violate the way God designed the human body. Performance-enhancing drugs are a shortcut to greater strength in the moment, but they can have devastating results in the long term. Putting rocket fuel in a car engine may create a very quick ride, but it will be short and leave you without transportation.

The human body was created with the potential for increased strength through weight and exercise training. The muscular system is continually maintaining and building itself up depending on what we ask it to do. Strenuous targeted lifting wears down a muscle, which the body then rebuilds a little stronger than it was before. Over time and with regular effort, significant increase of strength can be achieved. Those who have looked at the De LaSalle record of success over the years point to the consistency of having players who weight train throughout the year: developing teams that are not always the biggest beasts on the block but certainly the most conditioned players on the field.

On the spiritual side of things, being strong includes a built-in paradox. We become stronger as we realize how weak we are and how much we need God. In fact, the phrase "be strong" in today's verse actually means *be strengthened*. It means *get the strength you need from someone*. Paul knew very personally about this process. To the same group of Corinthians he would later write about a particular weakness he experienced. This bothered him a lot, and he really prayed about it. Paul wanted God to make him strong in that area. But God told him, "My grace is all you need. My power works best in weakness" (2 Corinthians 12:9a, NLT). Paul settled in to the reality of what he couldn't do because he realized that was where he would see God work the most. He wrote, "So now I am glad to boast about my weaknesses, so that the power of Christ can work through me" (2 Corinthians 12:9b, NLT).

On a team, you can't do everything. You must depend on the combined strengths of others to succeed. In life, God wants you to depend on Him in those areas where you are weak, and let Him make you strong.

When have you depended on God and found your strength in Him?

IT'S ALL ABOUT LOVE

And do everything with love
(1 Corinthians 16:14, NLT).

Maybe it's expected of a high school connected with the church, but people are often surprised when they start looking into the way De LaSalle conducts its athletic program. They are not sure what to think when they are told the school's teams make their main objective to love one another. Yet, the players' meetings that occur the night before a game are often less about a pep rally to pump everyone up and more about players standing and telling teammates how much they love those who wear the same uniform.

When Paul told the Corinthians to do everything with love, there was very little soft or shallow in the words he used. He was expecting Christians to love the way God loves, with a sacrificial attitude that really looks out for the other person rather than thinking about what they're getting out of it themselves. But it's the immediate context that really puts the idea of love in an interesting light. Paul had just told those believers to be watchful, stand firm in the faith, act like men, and be strong—all manly, testosterone-laden qualities that get us huddled up and doing fist bumps and high-fives. Then he says essentially, "All this macho stuff I just mentioned? Do all of that in a way that communicates love."

Until he was passed by Bruce Smith, Reggie White was the NFL sack record holder with 198 quarterback takedowns. He was a powerful, quick, and cagey lineman who gave opposing offensive linemen nightmares. His size was intimidating enough and his reputation seemed to make him look bigger. And yet, his nickname was "Minister of Defense." Off the field he was a soft-spoken, intense preacher of the gospel. On the field, a force of nature; but with a Bible in his hand, a man who loved people and spoke with great earnestness about the important things of life.

Authentic love gives way, but it isn't soft. In fact it can be hard and tough as nails. Jesus said, "There is no greater love than to lay down one's life for one's friends" (John 15:13, NLT). In one of the team meetings for De LaSalle, a player is struggling to describe how he feels about his teammates and he says, "I'd die for you guys on the field." Coach Lad has to correct him with, "You mean you'd exhaust yourself on the field—it's only a game."

Jesus not only said those inspiring words, He also went out and lived—or died—by them. He did lay down His life for His friends. He died on the cross for us, whom He calls friends even though we don't deserve it. John 3:16 tells us God sent His Son to the world because He loves us, which basically means that everything Jesus did had love as its motive. The more we can imitate Jesus, the more we will do everything with love.

How can you do today's tasks with love?

WHERE LOVE STARTS

In this is love, not that we loved God, but that He loved us and sent His Son to be the propitiation for our sins (1 John 4:10, NKJV).

We would make a huge mistake to think that loving God ever catches Him by surprise. He never waits for us to love Him before loving us. In fact, we first should recognize our situation before we even think about loving God. Until then, we won't be just ignorant of God and His love, we will actually be resisting and rejecting that love because we don't want Him messing in our lives. Romans 5:8 gives us a good picture of our predicament: "God showed his great love for us by sending Christ to die for us while we were still sinners" (NLT). We need a good dose of God's love before we're ready to consider loving Him back.

To accept the personal sinner label is not easy. We can easily say we're *all* sinners, but personal ownership is another matter, and we almost immediately start rationalizing: "I may be a sinner, but look at how much worse a sinner he is! By comparison, I'm much better." This only works until we realize the definition of sinner isn't a human pecking order; it's measured against the holiness and justice of God. The Bible declares, "All have sinned and fall short of the glory of God" (Romans 3:23, NKJV). Whether or not we fall short of ours or anyone else's standards doesn't matter as much as the fact that we fall short of *God's* standard.

God tells us we're in trouble because He loves us. If He didn't love us, we'd be on our way to hell without a chance. And when God gets through to us, we discover that He has already done a lot more than merely inform us of the uncomfortable news about being sinners. He has already done something about our sin. In today's verse, the word used is *propitiation*, which means "debt settlement." God sent Jesus to pay the debt for our sins. This means that Jesus took on the weight and the punishment for our sins in our place, so we wouldn't have to. Unless we let Jesus do that for us, we're stuck having to bear the eternal consequences of our sins.

God loves us and doesn't want to see that happen. Jesus shows us how much God loves us: He sacrificed His own life.

The Good News that the Bible brings us doesn't really sound like good news unless we realize what kind of trouble we're in without it. So the bad news of our sinfulness has to settle in before we're in the right place to accept what God did for us on the Cross as the best news that's ever been proclaimed!

How do you respond to God's Good News?

WHY IS LOVE THE GREATEST?

So now faith, hope, and love abide, these three; but the greatest of these is love (1 Corinthians 13:13, ESV).

Love isn't just love. It's not a self-defining word. Maybe that's why it gets used so much—it sounds good even when we don't know what it means. But when we read the Bible, we discover that God knows all about love and can teach and demonstrate it for us all day. When it comes to love, Jesus is the ultimate coach.

First Corinthians 13 is a popular passage from the Bible about love. It's often read at weddings. Here are the key verses:

> Love is patient and kind; love does not envy or boast; it is not arrogant or rude. It does not insist on its own way; it is not irritable or resentful; it does not rejoice at wrongdoing, but rejoices with the truth. Love bears all things, believes all things, hopes all things, endures all things. Love never ends (verses 4–8, ESV).

That list of qualities makes a pretty good case for love not just being about some nice feelings toward someone else. The first quality listed is being patient, which implies that the person we love is acting in some way that doesn't make patience automatic—because we love that person, we *are* patient. Note how many of the qualities of real love are about not acting in ways that often seem natural to us, like irritability, resentfulness, envy, and arrogance. That little sequence describing love as something that "bears all things, believes all things, hopes all things, endures all things" sounds like what we really need to make it through two-a-days and weight training! Really loving other people takes everything we've got.

We look at a list like that and if we're honest we'll say, "God help me!" Real love isn't easy. The love we are talking about is God's kind of love, not ours. If we are going to love others this way, we will not only need God's help, we are also going to need God to do the loving through us. That's exactly the amazing thing about loving God's way. It changes the people we love, but it changes us even more.

Notice that Paul ends his little explanation of love with a somewhat puzzling statement in verse 13: "So now faith, hope, and love abide, these three; but the greatest of these is love." It's not hard to think about faith, hope, and love as being very important aspects of life, but why would he say that love is the greatest? After all, according to Ephesians 2:8–10, faith saves us, and hope is the characteristic noticed in people who are on their way to heaven. So what makes love the greatest?

Here's a possible reason. In heaven, there will be no need for hope or faith. Our hopes will be realized and our faith will be sight. But love will always be there—it's the air of heaven. We might as well breathe as much of it as we can while we're here on earth!

Where do you need to show love today—and what characteristic of love will you call on to help you?

DEATH BEFORE LIFE

Most assuredly, I say to you, unless a grain of wheat
falls into the ground and dies, it remains alone; but if
it dies, it produces much grain. He who loves his life
will lose it, and he who hates his life in this world will
keep it for eternal life (John 12:24-25, NKJV).

The only way to know for sure you will never lose a game
is not to play in the first place. The risk of losing must be
accepted in order to play for the joy of winning.

Playing football well requires eleven players to function
at a high level of coordination—every member knowing and
carrying out his role while depending on ten other teammates
to do likewise. It also means recognizing when the other team
is not functioning that way and exploiting their weakness.
The loss of the freedom to do what you want to do in order to
contribute to the scheme of the whole team is a lesson Coach
Lad wants to impart to his team and must practice himself as
the coach. In the movie, when Coach Lad turns over the play-
calling to his quarterback during the last drive of the game, he
loses some of himself in the process.

The principle of "staying at home" when a play is going
the other way is a good example of losing something. If the
assignment is not to pursue the football but wait for the reverse
or the cutback, and a player makes the decision to pursue

anyway, he may succeed in a play. In the flow of the entire game, however, that independence will eventually be exploited by the other team. Good teams will accept a loss of yardage on a play if it reveals an opposing player who is making up assignments as he goes along. They will run one or more plays specifically designed to show how that player's attempt to demonstrate special *individual* strength can be shown as a weakness when met by a team in motion. Gap discipline and carrying out your assignment may not be personally rewarding on every play, but doing what you've been asked to do, even though it costs you something, will gain you trust with the coach.

When Jesus said, "Unless a grain of wheat falls into the ground and dies, it remains alone; but if it dies, it produces much grain," He was confirming a big lesson in life that is illustrated in small ways on a football field. By itself, a seed of wheat can't be ground into much flour. But if it is planted and "lost" in the soil, it will deliver heads of grain that can accumulate into the makings of a delicious loaf of bread. But the grain has to die and cease to be in order for the objective to be reached. An individual human life may have a small impact, but lost in the hands of God, it can have an amazing effect on the world.

What can you do to die to self?

FIRST STEP

No. Still way too slow. Blow off the ball, faster first step, and strike like you mean it.

—COACH LAD
From the movie *WHEN THE GAME STANDS TALL*

My dear brothers and sisters, take note of this:
Everyone should be quick to listen, slow to speak
and slow to become angry, because human anger
does not produce the righteousness that God desires
(James 1:19–20, NIV).

We often get the pace of things confused. What should be fast, we do too slow; when we should take our time, we hurry and mess things up. This happens everywhere in life, including our efforts to live faithfully for God. James uses that expression "quick to listen," and it almost sounds like a joke. Yet we know he's right. We don't listen fast enough. We don't pay attention until something smacks us and makes us realize we should have been paying attention sooner.

Most of us can also think of times when we spoke too quickly. We opened our mouths and said something without thinking and discovered that words can't be reversed. And what about anger: slow or fast? It may simmer into a rage, but anger itself usually starts with a spark. Just a look, a word, or a gesture can sometimes provoke an angry response. James is saying that getting the speed right is one way God wants to help us live the way He designed life to run.

All of this has to do with the right speed at the right time. The lesson applies to all areas of life, including the football field. In one scene of the movie, Coach Lad is training his linemen, using the sled equipped with pads that represents the opposing line. As if the sled itself isn't heavy enough, the coach is standing on the platform he expects his players to move down the field. He is looking for an explosive, coordinated push that will move the massive weight of the sled in a straight line, representing their opponents being driven back.

This is practice. The coach wants a level of preparation that looks and feels like game conditions. Most players can easily excuse lack of, or half-hearted, practice by thinking that once the whistle blows on game day, they will turn it on and do what they haven't been doing all week. Coach Lad has years of experience to back him up when he tells them that the way they are practicing will not translate to a great game because they won't have anything to turn on when they face game conditions.

We practice when the pressure isn't on so we can perform when the pressure *is* on! Think about James' three pointers: listen faster, speak slower, put anger in slow-motion. Practicing these habits in ordinary situations every day can help us put them into practice on those days when things feel like a pressure-cooker.

Where can you practice these techniques today?

BODY ARMOR

Therefore, put on every piece of God's armor so you will be able to resist the enemy in the time of evil. Then after the battle you will still be standing firm. Stand your ground, putting on the belt of truth and the body armor of God's righteousness. For shoes, put on the peace that comes from the Good News so that you will be fully prepared. In addition to all of these, hold up the shield of faith to stop the fiery arrows of the devil. Put on salvation as your helmet, and take the sword of the Spirit, which is the word of God (Ephesians 6:13–17, NLT).

When the Apostle Paul wrote this description, he probably was looking at a soldier in body armor. The Romans would send their infantrymen into battle wearing a set of protective gear that was light and flexible. He mentions a belt, torso body armor, shoes, a shield, a helmet, and a sword. Note that modern warfare has increasingly returned to the old-school model of equipping soldiers with significant personal body armor for combat operations.

Football players wear more body armor than athletes in any other sport. And the language used to describe a game often takes on military tones with teams in the trenches, battling it out, and occasionally throwing a bomb. The parallels between military and sports body armor aren't exact, but the purpose for each is—to keep someone in the action. Body armor doesn't prevent all injuries, but it does minimize many and allows participants to engage at a higher level than they otherwise would. Imagine the effects, in a football game, of a collision between the offensive and defensive lines with the linemen wearing no pads. Or how about a pad-less running back or wide receiver being hit full speed by a fully padded linebacker!

Life can be viewed as a serious game or as a potentially deadly battle. In either case, those who are wise equip themselves with protection when they engage. Paul was pointing to visible items of protection as reminders of real aspects of spiritual protection that God has issued to us. He mentions the truth belt, God's righteousness body armor, Good News of peace shoes, shield of faith, helmet of salvation, and the Word of God sword. Reading the list the first time, we may not even recognize the importance of some of the items. When first-time players and soldiers are issued their gear, some of it may look strange to them, too. But wise players, soldiers, and believers discover how each component works to keep them safe.

In the case of our spiritual armor, with the exception of our Bible, none of these tools is visible to the naked eye, but they are real and essential. The Bible becomes our source for discovering how each component in our gear should be used.

If this is new to you, make a list of each item and begin to create a description of how you can use each one in daily living. Your quest may take some effort, but the results will be worth it.

SACKED

> We now have this light shining in our hearts, but we
> ourselves are like fragile clay jars containing this great
> treasure. This makes it clear that our great power is
> from God, not from ourselves. We are pressed on
> every side by troubles, but we are not crushed. We are
> perplexed, but not driven to despair. We are hunted
> down, but never abandoned by God. We get knocked
> down, but we are not destroyed. Through suffering,
> our bodies continue to share in the death of Jesus so
> that the life of Jesus may also be seen in our bodies
> (2 Corinthians 4:7–10, NLT).

On passing plays, the offensive line is supposed to protect the quarterback by keeping the defensive players out, allowing the QB to stand in the pocket, scan the field, see the receivers, and deliver the ball. But the job of those defensive players is to get to the quarterback and tackle him in the backfield. That's a "sack." A player tackling the quarterback at the same time as someone else gets credit for half of a sack. The current NFL single season record for sacks belongs to Michael Strahan who had 22.5 in 2001.

In a game in 1966, Dallas defenders sacked Pittsburgh quarterbacks a record twelve times. NFL teams average about sixty offensive plays per game. If half of those are passing plays, you can see that getting twelve quarterback sacks in one game is a ton. That's exactly what the quarterback feels has landed on him by the time he is mercifully substituted.

What do you think Pittsburgh's second-string quarterback thought when he saw the Dallas tackles and ends pouring through the line? How about when the coach told him to strap on his helmet and get in the game? He was in for an adventure, for sure—trying to run the offense but running for his life instead.

We can feel that way at times. Somehow, some way, opposing forces keep breaking through, charging right at us, and knocking us flat. We know that will happen occasionally— but so many times, so soon? We get up, and then down we go again. A terrible argument with a friend. A last-second defeat. A lost prized possession. A lingering sickness. Just when we think we're in the clear, another one hits, and we're tasting turf. And sometimes the hits come because of our faith in Christ. We may even wonder how God could allow us to go through so much.

Just remember this: The true measure of a person's character and commitment is how that person responds to hard times. We know that God allows us to struggle and suffer for His reasons. We probably won't ever know those reasons while we're here on earth, so we just have to trust Him. And like those intrepid quarterbacks, we have to get up, wipe off the mud and blood, and call the next play. We may get sacked a few times, but we're in the game to stay.

What has you tasting turf today? What will help you get up and keep going?

IT'S GOLDEN

Therefore all things whatsoever ye would that men should do to you, do ye even so to them: for this is the law and the prophets (Matthew 7:12, KJV).

This is the Golden Rule. It looks and sounds deceptively simple: Do to others what you would like them to do to you. But as they say, if it were easy, everyone would be doing it.

When Jesus said these words, He wasn't inventing a new truth. Others had made similar statements. For example, one popular form of the Golden Rule was and continues to be, "Don't do to others what you wouldn't want them to do to you." Good thought, but it's only part of the way to treat others well. This "rule" simply tells us to avoid provoking others to retaliate against us. If we try to follow this approach, we end up with shallow relationships and a lack of positive impact in other people's lives.

Jesus' version pushes us to actively consider how we want to be treated and then treat others that way. It is a proactive approach, despite the fact that this way of building relationships doesn't come with guarantees. Most can think of circumstances in which they have treated others the way they want to be treated, but didn't get treated that way in return. Offering a hand up to someone you just tackled rather than leaning over and trash-talking doesn't mean they won't do just the opposite when the circumstances are reversed.

Too often, the way we tend to treat others might be described more like, "Do to others *before* they do to you." Which of course misses the point entirely. It expresses a cynical view of the world in which we are acting preemptively to make sure no one harms us.

Our biggest problems come when we turn the Golden Rule around and assume others should treat us the way we want to be treated *before* we treat them that way. If we expect others to always set the pace in kindness or gratitude, while withholding these things ourselves, we will be very disappointed. Someone has to start the process; why shouldn't it be you?

Does this approach guarantee that others will treat you well? No. But remember this: When Jesus said, "Whatever you did for one of the least of these brothers and sisters of mine, you did for me" (Matthew 25:40, NIV), He was giving us the best reason to always apply the Golden Rule in our relationships, even when people don't reciprocate. Treating others as we want to be treated also means that we treat others as we would treat Jesus Christ.

Where can you apply the Golden Rule in the next few days?

....

....

....

....

....

....

....

....

....

....

....

....

....

....

....

....

....

....

BETTER THAN YESTERDAY

> Then Christ will make his home in your hearts as you trust in him. Your roots will grow down into God's love and keep you strong. And may you have the power to understand, as all God's people should, how wide, how long, how high, and how deep his love is. May you experience the love of Christ, though it is too great to understand fully. Then you will be made complete with all the fullness of life and power that comes from God (Ephesians 3:17–19, NLT).

The Bible contains some great prayers. This one is worth memorizing and using for meditation. It really pushes the boundaries of our understanding of God's love by showing us that God's love *doesn't have* boundaries. Whatever direction we look—wide, long, high, deep—we never come to the end of God's love.

This prayer was first expressed by the Apostle Paul for the Christians in Ephesus. When we read the words, we can imagine him praying them over our lives. And if we learn the words, we can pray them over others. We want to experience all we can of the love of God and desire to see those around us experience that love, too.

Something is quite comforting and challenging about Christ making Himself at home in us. But it doesn't happen if we don't trust Him, and the trusting doesn't come easy. Fortunately, it only takes a mustard seed of trust to invite Jesus into our lives. From that point, as trust grows, His at-homeness grows in us.

This prayer makes clear that we will spend our lives learning and improving our trust in Christ and our experience of God's love. We will never get to the end of all God has for us in this lifetime. The picture of us being "made complete with all the fullness of life and power that comes from God" is the end result we will reach at the moment we enter heaven, not a moment before.

That doesn't mean we can't grow a long way, however. The whole tone of this prayer tells us that loving God isn't about us trying real hard to squeeze some love out of our dried-up souls. If we really experience the love of Christ and the height, breadth, length, and depth of God's love, we will discover love flowing out of us to others. We don't generate it; we simply receive it and let it flow on through. We discover, sometimes to our amazement, that we are loving God and others in ways we couldn't imagine before.

The transformation comes bit by bit. We catch a glimpse of this in Tayshon's life in the movie, starting out as an entirely self-centered person but gradually growing into someone who can see and care for others. That's the direction we should all be headed.

How can you let the love of God flow through you to others today?

_____

_____

_____

_____

_____

_____

_____

_____

_____

_____

_____

_____

_____

_____

_____

_____

_____

_____

_____

_____

CHARACTER MAKES A DIFFERENCE

The LORD said to Samuel, "Don't judge by his appearance or height, for I have rejected him. The LORD doesn't see things the way you see them. People judge by outward appearance, but the LORD looks at the heart" (1 Samuel 16:7, NLT).

Coaches call them the *intangibles*: qualities that make a player great but can't be timed with a stopwatch or measured with a tape. These characteristics are often discussed using terms like *vision, understanding the game, reflexes*, and *knowing what it takes to win*; but if greatness could be accurately quantified, every team would be stocked with superstars.

Intelligent players make stupid mistakes, and the fastest athlete on the team may be beaten on a play. It often takes a whole game, with all the odd ways the ball bounces, to reveal that combination of qualities certain players possess that can be called *character*. And character doesn't necessarily translate into winning the game. A player with character gives all he has and receives all he can get from any game. That's part of the idea behind Coach Lad's often repeated objective of having his players give a perfect effort.

So, why are the terms *leader* and *follower* benign (harmless, kind)? The answer begins when we realize leaders and followers don't function well alone. Leaders and followers need one another. Both leaders and followers can be good or bad in their roles. A team captain is not necessarily the best player. The lowest athlete on the depth chart may contribute the play that wins the game.

A certain level of ability may get you on the team, but ultimately your character will determine how you contribute to your team. In the film, Chris's dad can't see beyond the record he wants his son to break, but Chris is determined to make decisions that will see a bigger picture. His character comes through when he sets aside personal glory for the team.

Today's verse comes from 1 Samuel 16:1–13 when Samuel was sent to draft a new king for Israel. Jesse had eight sons. Several of them looked like royal material to Samuel, but God passed on the first seven. The eighth and youngest one, David, hadn't even been invited to the draft. But God told Samuel to go beyond the usual evaluation by appearance and height because, "The LORD doesn't see things the way you see them. People judge by outward appearance, but the LORD looks at the heart."

Clearly one of the reasons Coach Lad has developed so many excellent teams is that he goes beyond looking for talent and finds young men with heart, with character. He even helps very talented athletes see beyond their abilities to discover their hearts. Character lasts long after you've lost a step and are out of shape.

God wants to relate to you at the heart level. He wants to bring out and build the character He gave you. What are you like on the inside? How do you want to relate to God?

COACH

No one serving as a soldier gets entangled in civilian affairs, but rather tries to please his commanding officer (2 Timothy 2:4, NIV).

Bud Wilkinson played football and hockey at the University of Minnesota, earned his master's degree at Syracuse University, and served in the U.S. Navy during World War II. During his lifetime, he headed up President Kennedy's national physical fitness campaign, was a White House advisor during the Nixon administration, ran for the U.S. Senate, coached the NFL's St. Louis Cardinals, and served as a sports analyst and broadcaster for ABC and ESPN. But Bud is most well known for his accomplishments in college football.

In 1947, Bud was only thirty-one when he became the head football coach at the University of Oklahoma, and during the next seventeen years, he created a football dynasty. His Sooner teams earned a 145-29-4 record, including five undefeated seasons and three national championships ('50, '55, and '56). From 1948 through 1950, his teams won thirty-one straight games. Then from 1953 through 1957, they won forty-seven consecutive games—a national collegiate record. His teams also won fourteen conference championships and seven of nine bowl games.

Now that's a winner!

When asked the secret of his success, Bud answered that his players knew that they only had to please one person: *him*. He went on to explain that on many teams some players play for themselves to get glory. Others worry about their teammates. Some play to the opposition and get distracted by poor or dirty play. And, of course, some play to the fans, perhaps a favorite one or two. On Wilkinson's teams, however, players knew that what the fans saw or what the other players did was not important. All that mattered was what *he*, the head coach, saw, and how he evaluated their individual performances.

The Christian life is the same. We can become focused on personal stats or get distracted by other believers or the opposition from nonbelievers. We can worry about how certain people might think we're doing. But the only One who matters is God. That's who we're living for. We have an audience of One.

Today's verse uses the lifestyle of a soldier to remind us that active duty means focused living. We are under orders. A coach or an officer may demand our undivided attention, but our ultimate focus must be on the God who made us and has the right to speak into our lives. Ultimately, we're playing for Him.

Learn that lesson, live that way, and you'll be a winner.

What distractions keep you from staying focused on God and His will?

RUNNING THE ROUTE

Enter by the narrow gate; for wide is the gate and broad is the way that leads to destruction, and there are many who go in by it. Because narrow is the gate and difficult is the way which leads to life, and there are few who find it (Matthew 7:13–14, NKJV).

Jesus said these words when He was wrapping up the Sermon on the Mount. He was in that section of a homily or sermon that we call *application*. Everything He talked about in chapters 5, 6, and the first part of 7 were details of living as His followers. Now Jesus was beginning to give the disciples direction on how to put what He just taught into action. He still taught about bearing fruit and building the right kind of house, but here He talked about two paths for life: the broad way and the narrow way.

From what He said, it seems as though Jesus would not appreciate the way we use the terms *narrow-minded* and *broad-minded* today. In fact, His point was the direct opposite. We like the idea of being broad-minded, because it appeals to our "do anything, go anywhere, think anything" approach to life that actually leads to confusion. Meanwhile, we hear *narrow* and think *limited*.

Life brings many situations where limited is clearly better and more effective than broad. Think for a minute of the difference between a huddle where the quarterback says to the three receivers, "Run anywhere you want and I'll try to find you," and a huddle where the quarterback gives the signals that tell each receiver the precise routes he is expecting them to run. He expects to throw a pass to a spot on the field where the receiver and the ball will arrive at the same time—if that receiver runs the correct (narrow) route.

Considering what we believe and how we live, the broad way is doing what's easy, and the narrow way is doing what's right and true. Most people, in one way or another, are pursuing the broad way—doing what feels good and is popular. So, if you're just doing what everyone else is doing, you're on the broad way. But if you have decided to live God's way (and, by the way, the one that is right and true), you're on the narrow way.

The other part of Jesus' picture is important even if it is uncomfortable. He said the broad way leads to destruction, and the narrow way leads to life. Some people think, *I'm going to live any way I want, but I still expect God to make sure I end up with eternal life. I want to take the broad way to get to life.* But Jesus doesn't give us that option. He says the broad way is the wrong way. The narrow way, His way, is the only way that leads to life. So the question becomes, do you trust in God and His ways, or do you insist on going your own way? At this fork in life's road, choose wisely.

What evidence do you see of the broad way? What must you do to choose the narrow way?

REFLECTING

NO COMPARISON!

Pay careful attention to your own work, for then you
will get the satisfaction of a job well done, and you
won't need to compare yourself to anyone else. For
we are each responsible for our own conduct
(Galatians 6:4–5, NLT).

Isn't it amazing how easily we fall into the habit of
watching, critiquing, and evaluating other people and their
performances without giving much thought to our own? We
can stand on the sidelines or sit in the stands and analyze
what others are doing from the safety of distance. We're not in
the game. We're quick to think, *I could do that better*, knowing
full well we won't have to prove our words.

Comparisons are unfair to others and unfair to ourselves.
We feel as though we're coming out ahead when we find
someone with whom we compare favorably. It's as though we
are stepping on them to raise ourselves up, instead of paying
attention to our own shortfalls and problems.

When we realize that someone is better than we are,
we may subtly cut them down to size or we may become
demoralized and discouraged. However, it can be very helpful
to watch someone do a job well—especially if we need to do
that same job and we can learn from them. That's, of course,
why football players study game footage so closely. They

watch for mistakes, but they also watch for how the really great players play.

In today's passage, Paul is warning us away from the temptation to find fault with others. He does this by making two points that will serve us well no matter where we find ourselves in life or what jobs we do. The first insight has to do with the satisfaction of a job well done. We feel great when we step back after a project or an effort and realize we've done well. We've put together our past experiences, understanding, talents, and skills, and done better than we have ever done before. This is the life application of Coach Lad's principle of "perfect effort." It's that deep sense of completion that comes when we did everything we could, as well as we could, for as long as we could.

Paul also reminds us that "we are each responsible for our own conduct." We must be ready to answer for our choices and actions. We take a huge step into maturity and adulthood when we start owning our behavior. Comparing ourselves to others is one of the tactics we use to ignore (and get others to ignore) things in ourselves that need correcting. "Conduct" not only has to do with how we do our responsibilities, but also how we encourage and help others along the way. When we stop comparing ourselves to others, discouragement gives way to cooperation for the purposes of mutual improvement and encouragement. We take responsibility for our own conduct and move to a new level of teamwork and a deeper satisfaction in doing something well.

When do you tend to compare your performance to others in each of these areas: physical (sports, body, etc.); mental (grades, job performance, etc.); social (relationships, etc.); spiritual (closeness to God, spiritual disciplines, etc.)?

....

....

....

....

....

....

....

....

....

....

....

....

....

....

....

....

....

....

PROTECT THIS HOUSE

> Anyone who listens to my teaching and follows it is wise, like a person who builds a house on solid rock. Though the rain comes in torrents and the floodwaters rise and the winds beat against that house, it won't collapse because it is built on bedrock. But anyone who hears my teaching and doesn't obey it is foolish, like a person who builds a house on sand. When the rains and floods come and the winds beat against that house, it will collapse with a mighty crash (Matthew 7:24–27, NLT).

The words you just read are how Jesus ended His famous Sermon on the Mount. He had just covered a game plan for living, including various assignments and responsibilities. He warned about the opposition and what to expect as life unfolds. And just before He stopped speaking, He showed His listeners and us the choice we make every time we face the truth. He pointed out what everyone in His audience had in common. Although everyone had heard Jesus speak, He grouped them into two distinct responses: those who heard and followed His teachings and those who heard and ignored His teachings. Notice that Jesus didn't give the option to disagree with His words. Disagreement is a step we take on the way to ignoring what someone says. If a person is speaking the truth, our disagreement is wrong.

Beware of the tendency to put everything in the category of opinion. We know that everyone has a right to an opinion, so we can assume that one opinion is just as good as any other. We must remember that not all opinions are *right*. Consider this real-life situation. What do you think would happen if a coach stood up and laid out the game plan but ended his remarks with, "Now boys, that is just my opinion. You guys go out and do whatever you want to in the game because I know you have your own opinions about how things should go and they are just as valid as mine"? The result would be chaos.

Sometimes we don't want to know the truth because of the choice it will force us to make. In John 14:6, Jesus claimed to be the way, the *truth*, and the life. He never said we couldn't disagree or ignore Him and His words, but He clearly explained that our choice to agree and obey or to disagree and ignore would have consequences.

Choosing Jesus involves a big choice and a thousand daily little choices, like building a house board by board and nail by nail. Whether we are following or ignoring Jesus, we can build an elaborate house (life) that looks good—until the storms come. Notice that Jesus predicted bad weather for both those who ignore Him as well as those who obey Him. However, He added that only those whose houses (lives) have a firm foundation—on Him and His words—would weather the storms.

What are you doing to build your life on the solid foundation of God and His Word?

STREAKS

I know I'm not supposed to say this, let alone think it. But this streak is our legacy. We will never experience anything like this again in our lives. You are all my family but after tomorrow night, it will never be like this again. I'll never forget my time on this team or any of you. I love all of you. Spartans for life.

—MANNY GONZALES (quarterback)
From the movie *WHEN THE GAME STANDS TALL*

No, dear brothers and sisters, I have not achieved it, but I focus on this one thing: Forgetting the past and looking forward to what lies ahead, I press on to reach the end of the race and receive the heavenly prize for which God, through Christ Jesus, is calling us (Philippians 3:13–14, NLT).

Most football fans know about the New England Patriots' winning streak of 21 games that spanned parts of two seasons with a Super Bowl along the way. It doesn't quite match the Dolphins' perfect single season of 17 in 1972 that included a Super Bowl victory. The Oklahoma University consecutive win record of 47 included two national championships. But putting these amazing records alongside De LaSalle High School's tally of twelve straight undefeated championship seasons is not a fair comparison. Few other statistics offer such a sense of the power of a streak to inspire fear and admiration.

As the streak continued, Coach Lad always took the attitude that they never really concentrated on it at all. Instead, the team wondered what they could do each day to get better—how they could improve on their weakness—and that also included the offseason.

Life is a streak. Measured in seconds, days, months, or years, every moment of living is a never-before-faced chance to win or fail—to step forward or fall back. Yet, like a streak in football, we often live without considering how we're actually doing, where we're headed, and how long before the streak of life is over.

Streaks take care of themselves. Those not involved can think of a streak as the main thing, but every game, or in the case of life every *day*, becomes more important than the streak for the players. Unless the focus is on the immediate challenge before us, the streak isn't going to last anyway.

Spiritual living looks at every part of life as an opportunity to improve between games and between seasons. When the Apostle Paul wrote, "Forgetting the past and looking forward to what lies ahead," he wasn't talking about having amnesia about past experiences, but, rather, not letting the past have the last word on what we do in the future. The past has lessons that can be applied in the future. Paul was not trying to move forward while looking backward; he was leaning into the next challenge without being distracted by the previous ones.

As you extend the streak of life today, what can you work on to get better and improve weaknesses? How can you press forward to follow Christ?

ACCOUNTABILITY

I have Chris's card. Training commitment was ten extra tire drags after practice every day this week. Done. Practice commitment: one hundred percent ball security and pick up blitzing Sam linebacker on passing situations. Did that too. Game goal is two rushing touchdowns.

—DANNY LADOUCEUR
From the movie *WHEN THE GAME STANDS TALL*

Bear ye one another's burdens, and so fulfil the law of Christ (Galatians 6:2, KJV).

Coach Lad's use of commitment cards creates the settings for many teachable moments in the film and in real life. The commitment cards encourage personal goal setting. But Coach makes clear that a commitment card isn't just an answer to the question "What can I do?" It is a decision to go beyond what looks doable. The coach commends a card that has big targets that stretch his players' abilities. The commitment card becomes one way of answering the question, "What would it mean for me to put forth a perfect effort this week?"

One of the crucial uses of the commitment cards is their role in team building. The goals aren't private. Once a commitment card is written, someone else is asked to read it aloud to the team. Hidden goals can have a powerful motivating factor, but they are always subject to editing on the fly. Once goals are public, however, they can't be so easily changed. Others watch, encourage, cheer, and are themselves motivated by the effort.

Goals are special kinds of "burdens" willingly lifted on the way to accomplishing a journey. With no targets, the direction of the shot doesn't matter. With no destination in mind, arriving isn't really possible. But a De LaSalle player who writes a commitment card is setting out to carry a burden through the next game. And those who read the partner-player's card commit to helping that team member carry that burden.

The Bible's encouragement to "bear ye one another's burdens, and so fulfil the law of Christ" is talking about the significant team aspects of the Christian life. We follow Christ with others, not by ourselves. Commitment to Christ is personal and public. Just as the team sharing in Coach Lad's locker room is about more than game goals and individual challenges, the Christian life includes allowing others to know our burdens and discovering that brothers and sisters in Christ are willing to help us bear them. Ultimately, the coach wants his players to be able to tell and show each other genuine love. Christ wants the same thing.

So, what is this "law of Christ" mentioned in the verse above? When Jesus was asked, "Of all the commandments, which is the most important?" He gave a two-part answer: "Love the LORD your God with all your heart, all your soul, all your mind, and all your strength. . . . Love your neighbor as yourself." (See Mark 12:28–34, NLT.) The man who asked the question was basically trying to say, "What's your law, Lord? What do you say is more important than anything else?"

When we "bear one another's burdens" how does that fulfill Christ's law? The "one another" is just another way of saying *neighbor*. Which leaves the question of how bearing burdens for others is the same as loving someone as we want to be loved. This forces us to figure out the importance of knowing that others care, encourage, support, and want the best for us. Until we admit we need others' help, we're not likely to do much about bearing others' burdens or loving them.

In what areas of life do you need help?

REFLECTING

BEYOND WINNING

Marty (the reporter): *Bob, twenty-five years coaching this team, favored to win your twelfth straight championship. One hundred fifty wins. How d'ya pull it off, undefeated year after year?*

Coach Lad: *Winning a lot of football games is doable. Teaching kids there's more to life? That's hard.*

From the movie *WHEN THE GAME STANDS TALL*

That is why I tell you not to worry about everyday life—whether you have enough food and drink, or enough clothes to wear. Isn't life more than food, and your body more than clothing? (Matthew 6:25, NLT)

Marty wants to know the secret. He wants Coach Lad to spill the beans on the rare equation that leads to winning every time. The reporter in him thinks there must be a hidden explanation for the twelve championships, and his job is to find out and let everybody know. He has the same basic idea as the coach in the conference coaches' meeting who says, "There is no way someone can win one hundred and fifty straight games without cheating!"

One man's secret formula is another man's cheating. The first wants to find out the easy way to constant wins; the other is upset over someone else's success, assuming it can't possibly be fair. Both are wrong. Neither understands the point Coach Lad is trying to teach his players: Playing to win is worth the effort, but the game and life have much more to them than winning.

When Coach Lad used the phrase "there's more to life," he was echoing something Jesus said many times. Today's verse is the first part of a longer set of comments the Lord made about worry in Matthew 6:25–34. In a locker room, Jesus might have said, "That is why I tell you not to worry about everyday life—whether you will have a great game or come away with a victory. Isn't life more than performance and your significance more than winning?"

Ironically, Coach Lad knew that "winning a lot of football games is doable." Neither a secret nor cheating makes winning many games possible. And a very hard formula of perfect effort still doesn't guarantee the win. The reporter and the coach were worried about the outcome; Coach Lad was focused on the all that every game could accomplish. He knew he only had four years during which to influence the players in his football program, but he wanted to give them some tools that would help them through life and beyond.

Knowing that life is more than a game is a lesson that has to be learned repeatedly. Even Coach Lad, tackled by a heart attack, had to face the reality that his own life had to be about more than football. Ultimately, we have to keep learning the same lessons over and over. The coach's point about teaching being hard is simply that knowing what should be important isn't the same as *making* it important. And no one gets it right all the time.

Think of an area of life where what you know you should be doing isn't what you actually are doing. How can you make a necessary change?

WHEN ALL YOU'VE GOT IS FAITH

In Luke 6:38, Luke says, "Give and it will be given to you. A good measure, pressed down, shaken together and running over, will be poured into your lap. For with the measure you use it will be measured to you." Any idea what he's saying?

—COACH LAD
From the movie *WHEN THE GAME STANDS TALL*

So let's not get tired of doing what is good. At just the right time we will reap a harvest of blessing if we don't give up (Galatians 6:9, NLT).

In one of the brief classroom scenes in the movie, Coach Lad is leading a discussion on a statement made by Jesus, "Give and it will be given to you." Arturo offers his explanation: "You reap what you sow. Like, say a kid busts butt for his team, seems like God's message is, 'And for all his good measure of training so shall he be heaped with the same measure of playing.'"

The comments that follow between Rick Salinas, Tayshon, and Cam reveal significant differences in perspectives on personal actions and what happens as a result of those actions. Rick is trying to look at his current situation as a quarterback as a blessing from God for doing what is right. Tayshon points out that life isn't all that mechanical and can be very unfair. He doesn't see Rick's blessing as a result of actions but because he is tall and has a great arm. And when Cam speaks up for good things coming back around, Tayshon can only point out everything bad that has happened to Cam's family. But Cam responds with a quiet determination, saying, "It's gonna change. Everything I put out there, one day, it's coming back."

To which Tayshon asks, "What makes you so sure?"

Cam responds, "Read the quote, man. Luke is saying you got to have faith."

Tayshon says, "And you buy that?"

Cam quietly says, "It's all I got."

Before Tayshon can say anything else, Cam is called out of class to attend to his mother who is in her final days.

The discussion isn't resolved. Each of the players has a valid observation to make, but none of them (or anyone else for that matter) has the whole picture on what God is actually doing.

We can't figure God out except for what He tells us about Himself. And more is always going on than we can see. Those facts give us two places for anchoring faith. First, acknowledging that God still has options takes humility. And we need trust to realize that whatever is happening today is not the end of the story. If faith is all Cam has, he has a lot. But it will be tested (as it is in the movie).

The quality of faith isn't our small or great capacity to believe; it's really about who or what we are trusting and believing in. If our god is small; a big faith won't help. But if we believe in the Amazing One the Bible reveals, then even a little "mustard seed faith" in Him will take us a long way.

How would you describe your faith?

PUSHING THROUGH THE LIMITS

Cam: *Why is this happening to me, Coach? What'd I do? I'm trying. Makin' my perfect effort. But it ain't enough. What if Tayshon's right? Maybe God don't see me. Or He don't care. Cause I ain't worth His time.*

Coach Lad: *None of us can understand why things like this happen. We aren't promised an easy life. . . . But we are promised that, somehow, we'll see God use these things and this will all make sense.*

Cam: *It don't make no sense to me. I'm alone. Got nobody!*

From the movie *WHEN THE GAME STANDS TALL*

For our present troubles are small and won't last very long. Yet they produce for us a glory that vastly outweighs them and will last forever! So we don't look at the troubles we can see now; rather, we fix our gaze on things that cannot be seen. For the things we see now will soon be gone, but the things we cannot see will last forever (2 Corinthians 4:17–18, NLT).

Experiencing the death of a loved one changes how we look at everything. Cam struggles over the death of his mother, and Coach Lad will soon be confronted with his own mortality. They are both learning that each individual life is connected with everyone else. The choices and decisions we make can affect other people. But that doesn't mean that Cam's "perfect effort" will somehow prevent his mother from dying. Some days we may think that God can't see us or that He sees us but doesn't care. Having those thoughts doesn't make them true.

Something that is true remains true no matter how we feel about it. Being angry, happy, or sad about something true doesn't make it more or less true. Cam is having emotions and asking questions everyone asks when life isn't going as expected. We can wonder about God's love and care when things happen that hurt or confuse us. We may even conclude that if God did love and care for us, He wouldn't let us suffer.

If we decide that God must not see us, know us, or love us because bad things happen, we have a very shallow and shortsighted view of how love really works in relationships—especially in a relationship with God. A good coach puts the team through a lot of stress and pain because of what it produces in the players. If the drills were all easy, the athletes would not be prepared for what the game asks them to deliver. If practices aren't hard, losing will come easy.

God always has the long view. He knows what each person's life-season will take, and He doesn't hesitate to prepare us for it along the way. We may not like the training, but if we want to reach the end of the contest as winners, we will take the "present troubles" as part of God's plan and continue to trust Him.

What present troubles are you experiencing that you think God may be using to prepare you for the future?

....

....

....

....

....

....

....

....

....

....

....

....

....

....

....

....

....

....

....

NEXT GAME ISN'T LAST GAME

Danny: *T, we haven't lost a game in . . .*

T.K.: *I know the number, believe me. All I'm saying is open your eyes—your starters are mostly juniors and they ain't ready. On skills, you got half the team we did. On attitude, some got big heads, others just wanna wear the jersey and most think 'cause twelve teams ahead of them kept the streak goin' it's gonna be handed to them.*

Danny: *So . . .*

T.K.: *So you both got to step up, become real leaders, motivate your players to get even tighter than we were 'cause they ain't gonna win on just natural ability.*

From the movie *WHEN THE GAME STANDS TALL*

I returned, and saw under the sun, that the race is not to the swift, nor the battle to the strong, neither yet bread to the wise, nor yet riches to men of understanding, nor yet favour to men of skill; but time and chance happeneth to them all (Ecclesiastes 9:11, KJV).

No game and no season is ever just a *do-over*. Games and seasons aren't even "pick-up-where-we-left-off." Each one is a *start-over*. T.K. knows that Danny and Chris are in for a shock. He understands that when he, Cam, and the other seniors are gone, the whole team will feel and act very differently. He's preparing them for that reality, even though it won't hit until the team gathers without those who have contributed so much.

T.K.'s practical wisdom highlights the importance of seeing the way that abilities, attitudes, and assumptions affect a team's performance. He is pointing out to Chris and Danny that the team has a lower score in *all three* of those areas. The underclassmen have to prove themselves physically, several have ego problems, and all are in danger of thinking that a tradition of winning helps win games. Tradition can motivate; it can't make plays.

Solomon, the writer of Ecclesiastes, was a very wise man. He spent a lot of time observing life. He had the resources to try anything and everything. His wise statements aren't guesses; they are lessons from the tough school of life. He observes that races, battles, bread, riches, and favor don't always go to those whom we would expect. Other factors come into play, like time and chance. A game can turn on a gust of wind or an odd bounce of the ball—many factors over which the players have no control.

This is where T.K.'s wisdom scores. Danny and Chris *can* control certain things. Yes, they are new captains of the team—now they have to go out and *be* leaders every day. Those with the title of "captain" are expected to step up to the task of motivating, encouraging, and setting the pace for the rest of their teammates. They only have one season to do it, and they don't yet know that they would lose their coach for a significant time. These are the time-and-chance factors

Solomon observed. Real leadership comes into its own when it stays focused on what it can do and doesn't worry about what it can't control.

What leadership challenges do you face?

REFLECTING

THE EYES HAVE IT

Danny: *I've dropped more passes this summer than my previous three years combined.*

Coach Lad: *You're not looking the ball into your hands. You're turning your head up field before you've even caught it.*
From the movie *WHEN THE GAME STANDS TALL*

We do this by keeping our eyes on Jesus, the champion who initiates and perfects our faith. Because of the joy awaiting him, he endured the cross, disregarding its shame. Now he is seated in the place of honor beside God's throne (Hebrews 12:2, NLT).

A lot goes on in the film between father/coach Lad and his son Danny. The younger Ladouceur wants to experience both a father *and* a coach during his senior year of high school. This is a difficult balancing act to pull off for both of them. In this little exchange, they are exploring a fundamental about football and a fundamental about their relationship.

Danny and his dad can both see from the game film that he has developed a little habit that creates big problems in his main task as a receiver. In order to catch a pass, he has to "look" the ball into his hands. If he is looking elsewhere, like where he plans to go once he has the ball, he will probably not secure the football when it arrives. Running a great route means very little if he overlooks this one fundamental practice—keeping his eyes on the ball.

So much of football comes down to executing the fundamentals. Running, blocking, passing, catching, and tackling come with a thousand fine points and techniques, but they all start with a basic understanding that must be reviewed and practiced over and over. Knowing what must be done—like looking the ball in during a catch—doesn't mean much if a player doesn't actually do it.

The Bible explains that the life of faith includes the fundamental of "keeping our eyes on Jesus." Notice that the verse above calls Jesus the "champion who initiates and perfects our faith." What does that mean? The word *initiates* means that Jesus makes our faith possible. Belief doesn't exist in a vacuum; we have to have faith in someone or something. Jesus told His disciples, "Don't let your hearts be troubled. Trust in God, and trust also in me" (John 14:1, NLT). True faith begins when we put our trust in Jesus beyond anyone or anything else. The other word, *perfects*, relates to what Jesus does in our relationship with Him. Some Bible translations use the term *finisher*. In one sense this means that Jesus functions as our coach to bring us to the place where we are the best players we can be. When He *initiates*, He puts us on the team, but we are raw and undeveloped talent. His *perfecting* work in our lives is to coach us into being effective parts of His disciple team.

Our fundamental response to Jesus begins with faith and continues with faith all the way. We never get beyond having to trust Him, because every day brings new plays, new opportunities, and new challenges that require the basic practice of trusting Him, or as our verse today puts it, keeping our eyes on Jesus every step of the way.

What will help you keep your focus on Jesus?

....

....

....

....

....

....

....

....

....

....

....

....

....

....

....

....

....

....

WHAT'S YOUR RESPONSIBILITY?

It's a three deep and you got beat? When we're in three deep, you can't let them get behind you, Chris! Your responsibility is the quarterback on the option.

—COACH TERRY
From the movie *WHEN THE GAME STANDS TALL*

Blessed is the man who endures temptation; for when he has been approved, he will receive the crown of life which the Lord has promised to those who love Him (James 1:12, NKJV).

Tests are rarely enjoyable. Even when we study hard and know the material, something is grinding about waiting for the questions to be asked or the test sheets to be passed out. And some of us test better than others. A few feel like players who throw up before a big game. A coming test can get us so keyed up that the nervous energy disrupts our digestive system.

Tests are unavoidable, and they come in all areas of life. We can get in trouble if we assume that a test is designed to make us fail because, in reality, tests are opportunities for achievement and success. A test is supposed to us show what we know, not what we don't. The fact that we don't prepare well enough is what often makes a test a negative experience.

When James talks about temptation in today's verse, he is referring to testing. God doesn't tempt us; instead, He allows temptations into our lives to let us demonstrate growth and maturity under fire. God is not trying to trip us up or demoralize us. He wants us to develop a real-life capacity to keep going when the game is on the line. James says the goodness of blessings comes when we demonstrate we can stand up under a difficult situation and bear the load without getting distracted or discouraged.

Coach Terry is beside himself. De LaSalle players seem to have forgotten everything they have practiced. They are getting out-played, out-thought, and out-maneuvered. His instructions are reminders, not new information. They have planned and prepared for what's happening on the field, but his players aren't working the plan. They knew their opponent could present a deep threat on passing plays, so they stacked their defense three deep to counter the danger with multiple layers of tacklers. He can't believe they are still getting beat.

In his linebacker role, Chris can't lose sight of the quarterback during an option play because if the QB decides to keep the ball rather than tossing the lateral, Chris has to be ready to make the tackle. He can't worry about the fake to the outside runner. That guy isn't his responsibility. But if he tries to take on someone else's job during a play, his own duties will get overlooked. The opposing coach will exploit that lack of discipline.

If you know the plays the other team may run at you, and you expect that life will throw certain temptations and tests your way, you can be ready. What happens in a game will soon be over; what happens in life will last. Be ready.

What "tests" are you facing these days?

SHEDDING OBSTACLES

Beaser, this is just like the drill we do in practice every day. You've got to shed that block and get to the ball carrier.

—COACH LAD
From the movie *WHEN THE GAME STANDS TALL*

Therefore, since we are surrounded by such a great cloud of witnesses, let us throw off everything that hinders and the sin that so easily entangles. And let us run with perseverance the race marked out for us (Hebrews 12:1, NIV).

The writer of Hebrews wrote chapter 11 of his New Testament book on the examples of faith found in the Old Testament. Then, beginning in chapter 12, he puts his readers on the field or track in a stadium filled with a crowd of witnesses watching us from history and from heaven. He's not focused on winning the game; his attention is on technique. He says the race of faith involves several repeated moves: (1) throwing off everything that hinders, (2) shedding the sin that so easily entangles, and (3) running with perseverance the whole race.

Beaser is one of the heroes of the movie, a model for linemen everywhere. He's not huge, nor does he seem to be oozing with athletic ability, but he is teachable, and he rises to a challenge. The moment comes during an intense game where Beaser is having a difficult time handling an opposing blocker—a young man much larger and stronger.

Shedding a block is an important technique for a defensive player and one they need to practice and perfect. Some pros are famous for developing a signature move that others try to emulate. Reggie White was dreaded by offensive linemen for his "hump move" that relied on his speed, strength, and leverage. Watching him on film getting under an equal- or larger-sized player's arm and literally throwing that barrier aside usually provokes the question, "How does he do that?" Players like Reggie are technicians. They pay attention to the details in their sport and can break down a move into all its parts until they see exactly what works and what doesn't.

The phrase "everything that hinders" refers to blocks in our lives made up of good things that get in the way of better things. Not everything we like is ultimately good for us, and the pursuit of faith sometimes requires that we set things aside for a higher purpose. Beaser is kidded not only for having a knockout girlfriend but also for claiming they are practicing sexual abstinence. He's shedding a block of shortsighted selfishness to reach a goal of long-term freedom from regrets. Sins that easily entangle are temptations that seem harmless or even fun but damage our relationships and us. Tayshon is tempted to self-promotion and finds it hard to see how he's hurting the team.

Running *with perseverance* addresses our tendency to run out of gas, to give up along the way, and to lose sight of the truth that life, like a game, isn't over until it's over.

What blockers do you need to shed in your life?

SIGNIFICANT IMITATION

They're playing exactly like us.
—COACH LAD
From the movie *WHEN THE GAME STANDS TALL*

Imitate me, just as I also imitate Christ
(1 Corinthians 11:1, NKJV).

Imitation, as they say, is the greatest form of flattery. But it's more than that. Imitation is often part of the road to excellence. People who do things well usually find others who are doing things well and imitate them. Sometimes a good imitation surpasses the original. During the game, Coach Lad realizes that they are about to lose after 151 consecutive wins because their opponent is simply out-De-LaSalle-ing De LaSalle.

Learning from a negative example is much more difficult than learning from a positive one. Trying to develop a good habit from a bad example is a lot like trying to drive down the road at high speed while looking only in the rearview mirror. You can keep saying, "Back there is not where I want to go," but that won't keep you from eventually running into a brick wall. Plus, your driver's ed teacher will get really ticked at you.

Saying, "I don't want to play like *that* guy or *that* team" all day still doesn't describe how you *will* play. A negative example may motivate you to find another way, but you need a positive example to actually get you started in the right direction. So don't spend a lot of time watching people do it wrong; find someone who's doing it right and imitate that person. De LaSalle finally lost because someone imitated them well during a game when they didn't play up to their own ideals.

We can easily find people who say they are Christians but are messing up big time. We can call them hypocrites and claim we're not going to be Christians like them. But again, that attitude and perspective won't determine how we *will* live. Really getting serious about following Jesus Christ often makes you appreciate the efforts of others, even when they, like us, are sometimes getting tackled by life.

You probably know at least a few people who are doing a good job of being followers of Christ. You need humility and wisdom to say to someone, "Hey, I've been watching you, and you seem to know something about what it takes to live the Christian life. Would you tell me about it?" You may feel as though you're admitting failure, but you will find that the person you approach will probably thank you for the encouragement. He or she may not have thought anyone was paying attention.

Ultimately, Paul was right; we have to imitate people who imitate Christ. Jesus is the perfect example. We can study His life in the Gospels and get a lot of hints, but it always helps to find some people who have been imitating Jesus longer than we have and figure out if we can learn something from them. We usually can.

Who among your relatives, friends, and acquaintances is a good example of a Christ-follower?

CHOOSING NOT TO LISTEN

When I am afraid,
I put my trust in you.
In God, whose word I praise,
in God I trust; I shall not be afraid.
What can flesh do to me? (Psalm 56:3-4, ESV)

Courage is not the opposite of fear. The dark side of courage is cowardice. Coach Lad suggests three messages that the inside little voice whispers when people are afraid. Fear magnifies a problem or challenge (*it's too difficult*), it questions ability (*I can't*), and it undermines character (*I'm not good enough*). As he puts it, these are all voices we have to overcome.

A certain amount of courage comes through training. A new play in football that requires the coordination of several different players may appear impossible to pull off when it's described the first time. But going through the moves repeatedly increases confidence that the play can actually succeed! Also, the more we train, the more we will tend to do things without overthinking the steps, and we will be able to overcome obstacles.

Courage may also come from experience. We've faced challenges before that turned out to be less threatening than they first appeared. Experience teaches us to step up in spite of threatening appearances.

Courage is increased in teamwork and friendship. Something that looks so difficult we don't think we can do it because we're not good enough takes on a different look when we remember we don't have to tackle it alone. Knowing we just have to do our part can increase our willingness to ignore the voices telling us not to move ahead.

But courage is at its finest when it flows out of our relationship with God. More than once in the psalms we find people like David praying, "When I am afraid, I put my trust in you." Nothing is more effective in overcoming the voices of fear than trust in God.

Observe athletes today, and you will note that quite a few signal their awareness of God, pointing up during their celebration dance or crossing themselves at certain moments. But acknowledging God's presence and trusting Him are quite different. What do those same athletes do when they blow a play, drop the touchdown pass, or fumble the football? How do they indicate they are still trusting God even when things *aren't* going well?

Courage means trusting God whether we're alone or when everyone is watching. God is with us when we can't see anyone else, just as He is with us when we're surrounded by a cheering (or booing) crowd. We can know God cares when we are sitting by ourselves in front of our locker before or after the game, or when we are shoulder-to-shoulder in the huddle and the rest of the world is waiting. Fear shows up at almost any time and offers a way that is not courageous. We can overcome those whispers of fear by whispering this prayer, "Lord, when I am afraid, I put my trust in you."

In what situations do you need to whisper that prayer?

REFLECTING

LIFTING A TEAMMATE

Strengthen the weak hands, and make firm the feeble
knees. Say to those who are fearful-hearted, "Be
strong, do not fear! Behold, your God will come with
vengeance, with the recompense of God; He will come
and save you" (Isaiah 35:3–4, NKJV).

Isaiah, the ancient prophet of Israel, delivered a message
of hope from God to weary, crushed, and hopeless people:
"Strengthen the weak hands, and make firm the feeble knees."
When he encouraged others to be strong and not to fear, this
was more than just "keep going"; it was pointing people to the
help available in depending on God. Some waiting may be
involved, but God will provide help. He will bring salvation. We
need to be reminded of that truth in every circumstance, and
sometimes we need to find a way to remind others.

When you are concentrating on doing your best, you can
easily lose sight of the teammates around you. You may feel
as though you have all you can handle to do what's required of
you and don't have time or energy to help those around you.
If you stop to lend a hand, you may not be able to get going
again.

Is the objective just to finish successfully yourself or to
have as many successful teammates as possible? This is a

difficult question to think about when you're straining—which makes it the perfect question to think about right now. In an individual sport, you are not expected to look out for your fellow competitors, but on a team, crossing the line as a team with the slowest member may be a more significant action than straggling across one-by-one and leaving a teammate or two lost on the field.

What do you say and what do you do in the heat of the moment to help a teammate make it? Now is the time to decide because it might not come to you in the struggle. And what you actually say may be less important than the fact that you noticed your teammate struggling and that you are trying to help.

A consistent theme in the movie *When The Game Stands Tall* is the way players learn to look out for one another. Underclassmen hear about this but only when they are bearing the weight of the streak and preparing for the season do they discover the personal, hidden, and necessary part of teamwork—really caring for one another. In this small way, boys are becoming men who can lift the people around them because they understand at a deep level that others are more important than winning. They are also discovering what the prophet Isaiah and the people around him needed to realize— that God works in some of the most difficult times of life to bring about the best things in us and for us.

What can you do today to help a struggling teammate?

REFLECTING

THE TRAINING TABLE

Daniel was determined not to defile himself by eating the food and wine given to them by the king. He asked the chief of staff for permission not to eat these unacceptable foods. Now God had given the chief of staff both respect and affection for Daniel. But he responded, "I am afraid of my lord the king, who has ordered that you eat this food and wine. If you become pale and thin compared to the other youths your age, I am afraid the king will have me beheaded." Daniel spoke with the attendant who had been appointed by the chief of staff to look after Daniel, Hananiah, Mishael, and Azariah. "Please test us for ten days on a diet of vegetables and water," Daniel said (Daniel 1:8–12, NLT).

This wasn't a typical training table, but it had a definite purpose. The endless food line was a king's buffet. Every conceivable delicacy was included, and it was an all-you-can-eat buffet. All the food groups were represented, plus some never heard of. The grills sizzled with choice cuts, and tables groaned with tasty desserts. The king had been very specific about the diet his team was supposed to follow—his. He thought, *If they eat what I eat every day, how can they not mature into wise and amazing men just like I am?* Among those on the guest list for this royal dinner was a young man named Daniel. At this point, decades before he was dropped into a lions' den to become one of the Bible heroes, he faced a challenge that defined his life.

Daniel was probably high school age when he was taken captive by the armies of King Nebuchadnezzar and shipped off to be raised in Babylon. The king's plan was to select young men from the various nations he conquered and raise them to be wise men and counselors. So the kids with the highest ACT scores were gathered in Babylon for years of academic training camp.

Daniel was already old enough to know God well when he was drafted as a foreign exchange student. When he saw the king's menu, he noticed it was filled with items Jewish people didn't eat because God had told them those specific foods were not acceptable. Daniel didn't make a scene, but he quietly asked the head waiter for an alternative diet. He had very little control over where he was or the classes he was going to take, but he decided to remain in control of what he ate and drank. He was willing to cooperate with his circumstances, but he wasn't going to buy into the Babylonian lifestyle or lose his sense of personal responsibility before God.

As we see in today's passage, Daniel's determination put the friendly servant's neck on the line. Daniel wisely proposed a test: a trial period for his diet. By the time it was over, Daniel and his friends looked healthier than the rest of the gang, so they got to keep their diet.

Daniel trusted God and gave Him room to work in his situation. He did his part respectfully, and God came through in a big way. Daniel's early practice of staying true to God guided his long life and made him an example for generations to come.

In what areas of your life are you tempted to do what you know God would not want? How will you respond to those temptations?

UNDER FIRE

> Shadrach, Meshach, and Abednego replied, "O Nebuchadnezzar, we do not need to defend ourselves before you. If we are thrown into the blazing furnace, the God whom we serve is able to save us. He will rescue us from your power, Your Majesty. But even if he doesn't, we want to make it clear to you, Your Majesty, that we will never serve your gods or worship the gold statue you have set up" (Daniel 3:16–18, NLT).

Like the silent crowd in a stadium awaiting the national anthem, the huge crowd in Babylon stood silent, listening for the blaring horns. When they heard them, the crowd bowed before the towering golden statue of the king. The thundering sound of thousands bending their knees as they shouted in worship of the leader must have been heady stuff for Nebuchadnezzar. These were his people, praising him as a god. And why not? He held the power of life and death over them. Plus, as a little incentive, off to one side was a roaring furnace waiting for anyone who didn't hit the deck when the signal was given.

As the king basked in his glory, someone whispered, "Excuse me, Your Majesty. Three guys didn't bow."

Nothing is so irritating as thinking you're god one moment and being reminded you're not the next. Nebuchadnezzar didn't take the news well, but after summoning Shadrach,

Meshach, and Abednego, he gave them a second chance. They answered, basically, "All due respect, Your Majesty, but even though we are faithful servants in your kingdom, our ultimate allegiance is to God. If you force us to choose between you and Him, the choice is easy. We're going with God. We're not even worried about the furnace. God can handle it. But even if He decides not to, we're still OK with it. We'd rather die being faithful to Him than live knowing we disrespected the real God by serving other gods." The statement wasn't personal, but the king took it personally and had them tossed in the furnace.

They survived. The king got a clue that he wasn't God after all. And the three friends got even more leadership responsibility.

Whether the situation is the heat of competition or the fire of interpersonal conflict, life can present us with furnaces that test our real commitments. Will we buckle and go along with the crowd, or will we stand for what we believe, even if it costs us a lot?

In the movie this is the kind of challenge Chris faced between honoring and obeying his overbearing dad on the one hand and staying true to the ideals of teamwork and integrity he was learning from Coach Lad. Most of the time, he kept them separate, but eventually came the unavoidable clash. Even though Chris found it very difficult to stand up to his father's unreasonable demands, in the end even his father learned that his son's character was more important than his rushing record.

The fiery conflicts we have to deal with in life often don't seem to involve God directly, but He is always present. If we seek to honor Him in all we do, we can trust Him to take care of how things turn out.

What fiery conflicts are you facing today?

THE TIME TO LEAD

> Be strong and courageous, because you will lead these people to inherit the land I swore to their ancestors to give them. Be strong and very courageous. Be careful to obey all the law my servant Moses gave you; do not turn from it to the right or to the left, that you may be successful wherever you go (Joshua 1:6–7, NIV).

We tend to think of Joshua in the Bible as a young guy. As Moses' assistant, he was probably fairly young when he started out, but after forty years wandering in the wilderness with the people of Israel, even Joshua had some mileage. Now the time had come for him to take leadership of the nation. Moses was gone, and the people faced crossing the Jordan River and taking on the massive walled city of Jericho. They needed a leader, and Joshua needed help to be that leader.

God told Joshua to be "strong and courageous." Then He came back moments later and said, "Be strong and *very* courageous." Looking at what follows each of those statements by God, we see that leading a group of people into new territory takes strength and courage. But even more strength and more courage are needed to carefully obey everything God says. Ultimately, the road to real success has to be traveled with a significant amount of strength and courage.

When God says, "Be something," it's like when He was creating the universe and said, "Let there *be* light"—and light suddenly appeared. God doesn't tell us to be something He's not willing to help us be. He promised to give Joshua strength and courage as he relied on God. He wasn't asking the new leader of Israel to find it in himself; He was promising to supply what Joshua needed for the tasks He was asking him to do. He can still do that for anyone today who depends on Him.

The turn-over between Moses and Joshua took more than forty years. Significant changes happen every year on a high school team, and no one is around for more than four years. Because the window for success is relatively small, the learning curve has to be steep and the application efforts immediate. A student may not be the captain of the team, or even start on varsity, but he has many valuable lessons to learn along the way. More often than not, nobody knows where they will end up or how well they will play during their high school career. Their objective should be to become the best possible player that their skills will allow them to become.

It's that way in all of life. Become the best you can be with the skills and gifts God has given you. You can ask God for strength and courage, and you'll find that He supplies it in ways you can't predict.

Joshua didn't know what would happen each day and what he would need to manage it, but he was serving God. You can have the same attitude. You can be the best teammate possible. Be strong and courageous. Count on God's help to make this true for you.

What examples can you remember of friends, family members, or teammates being strong and courageous?

WAITING

Cam: *Don't make no sense coach. . . . I don't know what I'm supposed to do.*

Coach: *Stick to the plan. Go to Oregon.*

Cam: *Just don't feel right without him.*

Coach: *Please.*

From the movie *WHEN THE GAME STANDS TALL*

> Wait for the LORD; be strong and take heart and wait for the LORD (Psalm 27:14, NIV).

So much of life is about waiting. Waiting for our turn, waiting to grow up, waiting for what we hope will happen. We hate to wait! Maybe the hardest task before us is waiting for the Lord.

What is waiting? It's living through the period of time between the awareness that something will or might happen and it actually happening. But waiting also comes with feelings. If we don't want what might happen to happen, waiting might include a heavy dose of dread. If we are anticipating something really *good* to happen, waiting might be a joyful sitting on the edge of the seat. If we're not sure how we feel about what will happen, our feelings will be all over the place!

David tells us twice in today's verse to "wait for the LORD." One of the reasons this is difficult for us is because we usually make that phrase longer. We think, *Wait for the Lord to give me what I want,* or *Wait for the Lord to answer my question or solve my problem.* These thoughts come to us naturally, but they miss the point of waiting for the Lord, which actually means waiting *on* Him—anticipating how He will show up and what He will do. Frankly, most of us would rather have God do something *for* us from a distance than have Him show up and start messing with our lives. But that's exactly what David is telling us to do—not to wait for our wish list from God, but to wait for God Himself to show up!

In the movie *When The Game Stands Tall*, Cam has to struggle with the loss of his mother and his best friend, T.K. He has tried to be the kind of person God is pleased with, so he can't figure out why so many bad things are happening around him. He has followed Coach Lad's direction and filled out a commitment card of goals to pursue; but, in the light of his losses, nothing has made sense. In his frustration, he had torn up the card and thought it was gone. But we know Coach Lad had kept the scraps. When Coach said, "Stick to the plan," and pressed the taped-together card into Cam's hand, he basically told Cam to wait on the Lord.

Right at the end of the film, when Cam had some time to start seeing the bigger picture of his life, he realized that events happen for a reason. He knew that sticking with the plan was worth it. God does have a way to make waiting for Him worth our while.

What makes waiting difficult for you?

WHEN LITTLE GUYS STEP UP

I've seen it every year I've been part of this program. Smaller guys have been able to battle bigger guys because of their speed and willingness to hit.

—COACH LAD
From the movie *WHEN THE GAME STANDS TALL*

David replied to the Philistine, "You come to me with sword, spear, and javelin, but I come to you in the name of the LORD of Heaven's Armies—the God of the armies of Israel, whom you have defied. Today the LORD will conquer you, and I will kill you and cut off your head. And then I will give the dead bodies of your men to the birds and wild animals, and the whole world will know that there is a God in Israel! And everyone assembled here will know that the LORD rescues his people, but not with sword and spear. This is the LORD's battle, and he will give you to us!"

As Goliath moved closer to attack, David quickly ran out to meet him. Reaching into his shepherd's bag and taking out a stone, he hurled it with his sling and hit the Philistine in the forehead. The stone sank in, and Goliath stumbled and fell face down on the ground (1 Samuel 17:45–49, NLT).

This has to be one of the great action scenes in the Bible: David meets Goliath. Until that moment, everyone was afraid of the giant. He was an enemy too big to defeat, too strong to even face in battle. Everybody ran from him; the shepherd boy named David ran *toward* him. This is because David had a very different way of looking at the lumbering enemy who towered over him, trash-talking all the way. Where others saw an opponent too powerful to beat, David saw a target too big to miss!

David's pebble wasn't a lucky shot. He had practiced. Watching his father's sheep day after day had given him lots of time to hone his skill with the sling. The flock had faced real dangers in the form of wild animals that David was able to fend off with his weapon. So when the time came to meet Goliath, what looked like a mismatch was exactly the opposite.

For David, this whole episode wasn't a chance to prove how good a shot he was. It was a case of facing a superior enemy who had made the serious mistake of underestimating the power of Israel's God. Even before the victory, David gave the credit to God and let even Goliath know that God would have something to say about how their clash turned out. David wasn't going to take credit for victory. When God takes sides, all bets are off.

Coach Lad may not have had David and Goliath in mind when he talked about smaller players beating larger ones, but the principle holds true. Those who prepare for an apparently superior foe using their speed and willingness to engage often come out winners.

What "Goliaths" do you face? What can you do to defeat these enemies with God's help?

REFLECTING

AFTER A LOSS

*I truly believe that life's most impressionable lessons
are ones when something bad happens to you or
something challenging confronts you. I want to put it
in its proper perspective. This is football . . . and it's
fun and entertainment. That's all true. Nevertheless,
you were in a very combative and competitive
situation tonight. No one can climb into your head and
hear what that little voice is saying to you. Is it saying
"Oh no, we lost the streak"? What's it gonna say?
After tonight, you're gonna find out about yourself,
and you know something? We're all going to find out
what this team is made of.*

—COACH LAD
From the movie *WHEN THE GAME STANDS TALL*

Why are you cast down, O my soul? And why are
you disquieted within me? Hope in God, for I shall
yet praise Him for the help of His countenance
(Psalm 42:5, NKJV).

How often do you talk to yourself? Most people have an
internal conversation going on most of the time. We can be our
own harshest critics, and we can be our most unrealistic fans.
We can tell ourselves we're doing fine when we know we're
not, and we can call ourselves stupid when we really believe
what we did was just a glitch. The real question is, *Who are
you talking to when you're talking to yourself?* Or to think

about Coach Lad's statement above, *Who is that little voice inside you?*

David had a name for the voice: my soul. When you are talking, reasoning, and arguing with yourself, you are having an interaction with your soul, the center of who you are as a person. One of the amazing things about being a human being is self-awareness. But the soul doesn't get enough attention these days. How do you think conversations would go if instead of asking friends you meet, "How are you doing?" we asked, "How is your soul these days?" If this seems strange, think about these words of Jesus, "For what profit is it to a man if he gains the whole world, and loses his own soul? Or what will a man give in exchange for his soul?" (Matthew 16:26, NKJV). You don't want to lose track of your soul—it's *you!*

In today's verse, David noticed that his soul was cast down and disquieted. Sometimes we know why we feel the way we do; sometimes we don't. In either case, a healthy approach is to remind ourselves to hope in God. When everything seems to be falling apart, God is still there, and we can trust Him.

Coach Lad was talking to a team who had just experienced the loss that ended The Streak. The inevitable became crushing reality. He didn't want to try to minimize the moment by saying, "It's just a game," because he knew much more was at stake—the souls of his players. He knew that the loss and disappointment would give his team a much better chance of discovering who they really were than simply trying to keep a streak alive.

How's your soul these days? What can you do to remember that God is with you, even in the losses?

LOOKING UP

*I know what you do. I'm a teacher . . . I get it! But a
coach like you who knows the game inside and out
and teaches kids to become accountable, honorable
men, every school needs that. And you're brilliant at it.
I know; I've watched you do it since I was twenty-three.*

—BEV LADOUCEUR
From the movie *WHEN THE GAME STANDS TALL*

Jesus increased in wisdom and stature, and in favor
with God and men (Luke 2:52, NKJV).

Young people who read the Gospels the first time often
come up with a curious and frustrating observation: Four
accounts of Jesus' life and practically nothing at all about His
teenage years. Did He pass His first donkey-driver test? How
did He handle girls who were interested? How did He do in
sports? Did Jesus work part time in the Nazareth donut shop,
or did He always hang out at Joseph's carpentry shop as an
apprentice? Curious and inquiring minds want to know!

God has at least one very good reason why He arranged
for us to know almost nothing about Jesus' adolescent years.
Notice that every question asked by a young person is a
comparative question. They want to know how Jesus did so
they can tell if He had it easier or harder than they do. They
want to match grades and stories. They think about all the
temptations and struggles they face today, so when they read
a verse about Jesus like Hebrews 4:15, "For we do not have a

High Priest who cannot sympathize with our weaknesses, but was in all *points* tempted as *we are, yet* without sin" (NKJV, italics added), they wonder if it could be true. Did Jesus go through stuff that makes Him able to understand what anyone is going through? The Bible answers, "Yes."

God's Word doesn't give us the details of Jesus' teenage years, but it does give us a brilliant summary that's even better. It offers today's young people what they really need to compare their lives with Jesus' experience and figure out how they are doing in their responsibility to grow up. In today's verse, Luke wrote, "Jesus increased in wisdom and stature, and in favor with God and men." Notice these are four ways everyone should grow up, and the years in high school are prime maturing time.

Wisdom is your development of knowledge and how to use it well, sharpening your thinking skills, asking questions when you don't know rather than faking it. *Stature* is simply physical development, but it can also relate to the way your physical growth affects the other areas. The stronger you become, the more you can participate in carrying others' loads. *Favor with God* summarizes a person's healthy spiritual development. Jesus spent time with His Father; He also knew and applied the Scriptures. And *favor with men* relates to positive relationships with the people in His life. Some of these are going to be challenging.

In the movie *When The Game Stands Tall*, we see Tayshon, Danny, and Chris all growing in wisdom, stature, and in favor with people. The favor with God part is less apparent, but it is hinted at in the way they accepted Coach Lad's guidance even when it conflicted with their self-interests.

In order to really grow, you have to discover that a will greater than your own exists—God's.

How are you growing in each of these areas: mental, physical, spiritual, and social?

....
....
....
....
....
....
....
....
....
....
....
....
....
....

BEYOND EXHAUSTION

*We tied. And I have never been prouder of a team.
For ninety-three plays straight you delivered a perfect
effort. You grew up and became a team again. And
you know what? Growing up is painful. It's not easy.
But that's what our program is about, in case you
haven't figured it out. It ain't about the football. It ain't
about scoring touchdowns. It's about moving you in a
direction that can assist you and help you to grow up
. . . so that when you take your place out in the world
and out in our community, you can be depended on.*

—COACH LAD
From the movie *WHEN THE GAME STANDS TALL*

Even youths grow tired and weary, and young men
stumble and fall; but those who hope in the LORD
will renew their strength. They will soar on wings like
eagles; they will run and not grow weary, they will
walk and not be faint (Isaiah 40:30–31, NIV).

Isaiah had a way of saying things that sticks with us. He
could show us what is obvious and also what it means. Just
about the time we are nodding our heads in agreement that
sometimes even strong youths reach the end of their rope and
are exhausted, he adds a "but." Maybe you've been one of
those young men who thought they could handle a situation,
and then you eventually stumbled and fell. At that point,

who you are, what you know, and *who* you know make all the difference. Isaiah points to "those who hope in the Lord" as people who have something beyond natural strength to carry on.

Isaiah believed in spiritual conditioning just as much as Coach Lad and his assistants believed in physical and mental conditioning. Notice that even young people who "hope in the Lord" can grow tired, get weary, stumble, and fall. It happens to everyone eventually. At the end of human capacity and resources is where "hope in the Lord" makes the difference and renews strength.

Different kinds of strength (physical, mental, psychological, and even spiritual) are part of us like fuel. Situations tap our supply. If we are not renewing and replenishing our supply of strength, we will eventually come up empty. Resting and a good meal renew and replenish our bodies. Hoping in the Lord, engaging in prayer, and immersing ourselves in God's Word renew the soul. Eagle-like soaring and tireless running is up ahead.

After The Streak had ended and the team suffered several losses, a moment of truth came, described in Coach Lad's words above. Though his players had done everything they could in a game, they had only tied. They were spent. To the team, it felt like a loss; to the coach, it was a beautiful example of a perfect effort—what he had been trying to teach them all along. As he puts it, "It's about moving you in a direction that can assist you and help you to grow up . . . so that when you take your place out in the world and out in our community, you can be depended on." The perfect effort isn't just what you do; it's what happens *to you* along the way that really counts.

How will you renew your soul today?

PUSHING THROUGH PAIN

Danny (breathing hard): *I . . . can't. . . . He's gonna . . . go . . . forever.*

Luis (winded): *No, just . . . a little . . . more . . . than you.*
From the movie *WHEN THE GAME STANDS TALL*

Dear brothers and sisters, when troubles of any kind come your way, consider it an opportunity for great joy. For you know that when your faith is tested, your endurance has a chance to grow. So let it grow, for when your endurance is fully developed, you will be perfect and complete, needing nothing. If you need wisdom, ask our generous God, and he will give it to you. He will not rebuke you for asking (James 1:2–5, NLT).

Endurance, James tells us, is faith stretched out. Troubles are not fun, but today's passage tells us the best way to handle them is by considering hard times an "opportunity for great joy." If we've gone through some difficulties, this instruction can sound a little crazy. How can trials and suffering be a cause for joy?

Our question implies that we assume troubles create an opportunity for something else. What are our typical reactions to hardship? We complain, we resist, and we resent.

The kind of endurance James is talking about doesn't take troubles lightly. Endurance doesn't say, "Isn't this fun?" except when making a joke. Healthy endurance keeps the thought in mind that, at some point, we will look back at what's happening and it will make sense in a way that doesn't right now. Endurance can also think, *I've seen others go through this and I know how they turned out. I'm hanging in there for the same result.*

So, what is endurance? It's the attitude Luis, the injured veteran, has on the treadmill: "I don't have to go forever, just a little longer than this challenge." Endurance only stops when the need to keep going is over. The word translated *endurance* literally means "to stand up under the weight." The picture is a weightlifter holding a massive load in the air for as long as it takes.

When it comes to having weights of different kinds dropped on our lives, our instinct is to duck out or drop the bar. Endurance stays under and takes the weight.

Part of our problem with James' wisdom is that we confuse joy with happiness. Joy is deeper, wider, and longer than happiness. Happiness is what happens to us, and we can't always predict when it's going to happen and how long it will last. Happy feelings come and go. They evaporate quickly and we're left flat.

Joy is a settled sense that God is in control and life is going somewhere, even if the current circumstances are difficult. Joy takes the harder way and increases as life becomes fuller and more meaningful, including lots of moments of unexpected happiness, even though that wasn't what we were actually aiming for.

What troubles are you facing? How can you turn those into opportunities for joy?

MANAGING THE CLOCK

Coach Lad: *Salinas, this is your final drive as a Spartan.*

Manny Salinas: *Coach?*

Coach Lad: *It's yours. You call the plays.*
From the movie *WHEN THE GAME STANDS TALL*

Look carefully then how you walk, not as unwise but as wise, making the best use of the time, because the days are evil (Ephesians 5:15–16, ESV).

When the Bible talks about *walking*, we can almost always assume it's talking about *living*. So when Paul wrote to the Ephesians about being careful how they walked, he wanted them to pay attention to decisions they were making and what was going on around them. The phrase we want to focus on is "making the best use of the time" because it's a point of wisdom that we can apply in every area of life. Despite bad stuff going on around us and the days being "evil," we can still use our time well.

Regarding time, the most important decisions involve knowing what we should be doing right now in life. Solomon summarized the changing uses of time in his famous statement in Ecclesiastes 3:1–8:

> To every thing there is a season, and a time to every purpose under the heaven: A time to be born, and a time to die; a time to plant, and a time to pluck up that which is planted; a time to kill, and a time to heal; a time to break down, and a time to build up; a time to weep, and a time to laugh; a time to mourn, and a time to dance; a time to cast away stones, and a time to gather stones together; a time to embrace, and a time to refrain from embracing; a time to get, and a time to lose; a time to keep, and a time to cast away; a time to rend, and a time to sew; a time to keep silence, and a time to speak; a time to love, and a time to hate; a time of war, and a time of peace (KJV).

This list of times reminds us that we can do certain things at certain times, and if we miss or squander the opportunity, it's gone. Coach Lad and his son, Danny, struggle to connect as father and son while both are realizing that a very special opportunity is passing by. You have certain responsibilities and opportunities before you right now that may not be there tomorrow or in five years. Those are the matters where you can make the best use of your time. Are you in school? Then it's the time to be all there and making it the right kind of priority. When you are thirty, you don't want to look back and wish you had made better use of your time while in high school.

When you have made good use of your time, unexpected opportunities will come your way. That possibility is illustrated in the movie *When The Game Stands Tall* as the championship game is winding down and Coach Lad gives Salinas the privilege of calling his own plays on the final drive. The coach is rewarding excellent attitude and work ethic in one of his players by expanding his responsibilities in a new way.

Special times can come up just that quickly. What opportunities is God giving you right now to make the right decisions for His glory?

REFLECTING

....

....

....

....

....

....

....

....

....

....

....

....

....

....

....

....

RECOVERING FROM DISAPPOINTMENT

I've always believed that our greatness wouldn't be revealed until the streak ended. Well, this is it. Your year. You can be the team that lost the streak or the one that fought to come back from it. Be that team. Show the true heart and soul of De LaSalle.

—COACH LAD
From the movie *WHEN THE GAME STANDS TALL*

We have this treasure in jars of clay, to show that the surpassing power belongs to God and not to us. We are afflicted in every way, but not crushed; perplexed, but not driven to despair; persecuted, but not forsaken; struck down, but not destroyed; always carrying in the body the death of Jesus, so that the life of Jesus may also be manifested in our bodies (2 Corinthians 4:7–10, ESV).

Two basic ideas can help us approach the ins and outs and ups and downs of life. We either try or we train. When we think about today or about tomorrow, we can take the in-training approach or the trying approach. This may not seem like a big deal, but it can make all the difference when we face losses, failures, and disappointments.

The Apostle Paul knew a little about struggles and hard times. He didn't consider himself a tough guy. In fact, in today's passage, he calls himself (and us) jars of clay—breakable, fragile. If we think we're hot, tough stuff, then we can't see how much we need God's help along the way. In contrast, those who want their lives to count for God will simply accept the fact that the more they learn to be humble about their abilities, the more the surpassing power of God will be apparent to others.

Notice, however, what Paul says these jars of clay will be able to survive. "Afflicted in every way, but not crushed" means pounded but not cracking. "Perplexed, but not driven to despair" means we don't always know what's going on and why, but we don't give up. "Persecuted, but not forsaken" refers to people giving us a hard time about our faith, but we trust that God is still with us. "Struck down, but not destroyed" means when we get tackled hard, we get back up. Most clay jars would crack and crumble in those kinds of conditions— unless they have something on the inside. And that's the secret to enduring and even thriving in tough times.

What's the difference between *trying* and *training?* When we try, we get to quit as soon as we fail. Trying only requires one failure, and then we can say, "I tried." When we're in training, however, failure is part of the process. Training assumes many failures before we get it right. Successful people have had to overcome failures. Even after a winning streak of 151 games, as Coach Lad put it so well, the real test came when failure reared its ugly head. That's when the De LaSalle team discovered what it was really made of.

Failure does the same for us. It shows us what we're made of. We can be people who fail and quit, or we can be people who fail and recognize we've got to train harder.

What does "training" mean to you?

....

....

....

....

....

....

....

....

....

....

....

....

....

....

....

....

....

....

....

....

FINDING YOUR IDENTITY

The players are handpicked, self-motivated, smart, eyes fixed on their bright futures—they don't need what I do.

—COACH LAD
From the movie *WHEN THE GAME STANDS TALL*

Command and teach these things. Let no one despise you for your youth, but set the believers an example in speech, in conduct, in love, in faith, in purity. Until I come, devote yourself to the public reading of Scripture, to exhortation, to teaching. Do not neglect the gift you have, which was given you by prophecy when the council of elders laid their hands on you. Practice these things, immerse yourself in them, so that all may see your progress (1 Timothy 4:11–15, ESV).

The Apostle Paul was writing to a young disciple named Timothy, coaching him on how to carry out his assignments and how to live his life. The two of them had been part of a larger group led by Paul that had travelled throughout the eastern Mediterranean and southern European countries telling people about Christ and starting churches. Later, Paul sent Timothy back to some of those churches to help them stay on track with God.

Timothy was still fairly young when he embarked on his own, and Paul recognized that Timothy needed a lot of encouragement along the way. Paul hints in his letters about Timothy's timid nature and fears. But the positive words he used for Timothy help us see the apostle's concern for his young disciple's overall well-being and maturity. In today's passage, Paul spells out five personal areas that affect people around us when we are trying to communicate the faith and be authentic followers of Jesus. These are speech, conduct, love, faith, and purity. What we say, how we act, how we love, how we believe, and how we are real make a difference for others.

This list of Paul's moves in two directions: increasing impact and decreasing audience. More people are touched by what you say than get a chance to watch *closely* what you do. Progressively smaller groups experience your love, understand your faith, and finally get to know you at the pure or transparent level, which is more about honesty than about perfection. At the same time, however, the lasting impact and power of each of these areas increases. Your words may be forgotten quickly, but your actions will leave a longer impression. Those who move closer to you to be loved will grasp your faith and know the real you . . . and, with each step, be more deeply affected. Timothy's mission had formal aspects, but the main point was to become the kind of person God uses to help transform other people.

In the film, Coach Lad is considering offers to coach at a higher level with more pay and prestige. The financial security appeals to him, but he understands his passion to work with young men who are still being formed. He knows that high school is where he can work best. College coaching, in his view, is a very different arena. Coach knows that he fits where he is, even though the circumstances aren't perfect. He deeply believes that he is in a place where, in Paul's words,

his speech, actions, love, faith, and transparency can make a
lasting impact on the lives of young men.

What can you do to positively impact younger believers
and teammates?

....

....

....

....

....

....

....

....

....

....

....

....

....

....

....

....

MAKING PROGRESS

Mickey Ryan (Chris's dad): *You people . . . you don't understand the first thing about football!*

Bev Ladouceur: *It was never about football.*

Mickey Ryan: *Your husband just cost my boy his record.*

Bev Ladouceur: *My husband just turned your boy into a man. And everybody in this stadium knows it but you.*

From the movie *WHEN THE GAME STANDS TALL*

Be diligent in these matters; give yourself wholly to them, so that everyone may see your progress. Watch your life and doctrine closely. Persevere in them, because if you do, you will save both yourself and your hearers (1 Timothy 4:15–16, NIV).

People who make real progress always do better in the long run than people who aim at perfect performance. The difference is highlighted in the film, *When The Game Stands Tall,* by the coach's insistence that his players strive for a perfect *effort* over a perfect performance. He knows performance can always be improved, but in any given game, a player can produce a complete effort that deserves the title "perfect."

When the Apostle Paul instructed Timothy about ministry, like a good coach, he knew his player would be tempted to measure up to other people's expectations and reach for unattainable perfection. That's why he advised, "Be diligent in these matters; give yourself wholly to them, so that everyone may see your progress." Diligence and giving yourself wholly to something are perfection of effort, not perfection of achievement. Paul understood a fact of life: When we try to be perfect, the people around us can spot where we fall short in about five seconds. If we make claims about ourselves that we can't live up to—*I'm the best; I've really changed; I've got this all figured out*—others almost always feel compelled to knock us down and help us see the truth. When we over-promise or make well-intentioned commitments that we can't meet, people notice those failures in a negative way.

Instead, aiming for perfect *effort* includes the understanding that we always have room for improvement. When we are making real progress, people will notice in a positive way. People who have gotten better make a definite impression. For Danny, the coach's son, being able to hang on to passes more often and in crucial situations is an amazing achievement. He has been diligent and given himself to this task, and everyone sees his progress.

In the movie Coach Lad's wife and Mickey Ryan have two very different views of Chris Ryan. The dad can only see a perfect new record that can't be taken away and should be pursued at all cost, even the integrity and soul of his son. Coach Lad's wife (and everyone else) can see Chris maturing into a real man who can perform at a high competitive level but wants his efforts to be about more than his reputation or fame. He's willing to forego the perfect achievements in exchange for a deeper and more fulfilling perfect effort. His father finally gets this when it's almost too late.

If asked, what would those who know you best say about your efforts versus your performance?

....

....

....

....

....

....

....

....

....

....

....

....

....

....

....

....

FATHERS AND SONS

Oh Buddy, if you only knew. It seems like ten minutes ago you were sitting on my lap watching Daddy from the sidelines, and I could feel you dreaming of being the player he'd grab by the scruff when the pressure was on and send in to save the game. And now you're here. And you're putting all this pressure on yourself to deliver.

Just trust yourself as a player and do it for the guys and for the game, but you don't need to do it for him—to win his love. That guy, as awkward as he is at showing it? You've had him the whole time.

—BEV LADOUCEUR (Danny's mom)
From the movie *WHEN THE GAME STANDS TALL*

Fathers, do not embitter your children, or they will become discouraged (Colossians 3:21, NIV).

Two father-son relationships contribute significantly to the storyline and impact of the film, *When The Game Stands Tall*. Coach Lad has his son Danny on the team; Mickey Ryan has his son Chris (a star running back) on the team, nicknamed "Beast." Danny is desperately trying to contribute to the team and experience the complicated relationship of having a dad and coach who are the same man. Chris is closing in on the state record for most touchdowns scored in a high school career, and his father is fixated on that prize—demanding that his son achieve it no matter what.

Today's verse is simple, direct guidance for dads. It isn't about how much you say or how much you do together; it's about a father understanding what will make his son or daughter bitter and discouraged. This is about neglect. Fathers need to be deeply committed—not to a certain plan of attention to their kids but to just plain old attention of some kind to their kids. Counselors say that children misbehave not so much because they enjoy being bad but because they are looking for attention. Fathers' words and actions carry a lot of weight with their kids, even in small quantities.

The Bible is filled with stories of fathers and sons. Obviously, every person in the Bible had a father. All of them had some kind of relationship with that father as well, but many of those relationships were not positive. At the center of the Bible is the relationship with Jesus and His Father. We know Jesus talked often to His Father; we don't know how much the Father said to the Son, except for a few public occasions when God the Father spoke about His Son and others heard. For example, when Jesus was transfigured, God said, "This is my beloved Son, with whom I am well pleased. Listen to him" (Matthew 17:5, ESV). God the Father made three statements to Jesus that every child longs to hear from Dad: "I love you, I'm proud of you, and you are capable." A father cannot go wrong imitating God the Father in what he says to his children.

Sometimes another person, like Danny's mom, Bev, is needed to show a child that Dad's lack of specific words or actions don't mean lack of love. Sometimes a son like Chris is never sure whether his father loves him or his achievements. Ultimately, dads must bear the weight for delivering what their children really need—them. Regardless of your relationship with your earthly father, your heavenly Father is near, and He loves you.

How do you get along with your dad? How's your relationship with the Father?

REFLECTING

....

....

....

....

....

....

....

....

....

....

....

....

....

....

....

....

EXPLANATIONS

Reporters. Friends. Family. Strangers. Are all gonna ask you, "What happened?" It's a question that's going to follow you—"How'd you lose The Streak?" And your answer every time? The truth. Bellevue played better than us. And we lost a high school football game. That's football . . . but it's not you. Don't let a game define you. Let the way you live your life do that.

—COACH TERRY
From the movie *WHEN THE GAME STANDS TALL*

Do not lay up for yourselves treasures on earth, where moth and rust destroy and where thieves break in and steal; but lay up for yourselves treasures in heaven, where neither moth nor rust destroys and where thieves do not break in and steal. For where your treasure is, there your heart will be also (Matthew 6:19–21, NKJV).

Earthly treasures come in many forms: money, winning records, stock portfolios, public recognition, possessions, etc. The one thing all earthly treasures share in common is their vulnerability. They can be gone in a second, stolen overnight, burned in a flash. Most of the stuff we work very hard to get turns out to be stuff that's very easy to lose.

Jesus wasn't arguing against working hard, saving, and having things. He was warning us not to try to make the things that are temporal into eternal treasures. He was telling us not to rest our identity and our destiny on things that can't bear that weight for a second. All it takes is a tornado, a market crash, or a bad game to show us that what looked so solid and lasting really wasn't. Coach Terry made the same point in a limited way when he addressed the team after the loss that ended The Streak: "Don't let a game define you. Let the way you live your life do that."

We often hear the statement made about a particular achievement, "No one can ever take that away from you." Really? Yes, you will always be known as the champion for that moment or those years; and unless it turns out you were cheating, you will always be in the record books. But two days or two decades later, how much will having that achievement really matter in the light of eternity? After death, we're not going to talk about the stuff we left behind on earth; we'll talk about the stuff, as Jesus put it, we laid up for ourselves in heaven.

Jesus didn't give a list of heavenly treasures at that point, but a few verses later He indicated the difference between living a life limited to the earth and living a life with heaven in mind: "For after all these things the Gentiles seek. For your heavenly Father knows that you need all these things. But seek first the kingdom of God and His righteousness, and all these things shall be added to you" (Matthew 6:32–33, NKJV). Everyone has to seek after and deal with the stuff of life: working, playing, eating, marrying, raising kids, saving money, buying houses, and so forth; but some of us don't settle. We're seeking God's Kingdom and His righteousness because we know a life in God deposits treasure in heaven. As Coach Terry put it, "We're letting the way we live our lives define who we are."

What does it mean to you to deposit treasures in heaven?

REFLECTING

RIDING THE BENCH

I've been on this team for four years. And never once played in a varsity game. I'm not good enough. And that's okay. Because the greatest moments of my life were the times I spent on this team with you guys. I have never been prouder of anything than being a Spartan.

—ARTURO
From the movie *WHEN THE GAME STANDS TALL*

Whatever gain I had, I counted as loss for the sake of Christ. Indeed, I count everything as loss because of the surpassing worth of knowing Christ Jesus my Lord. For his sake I have suffered the loss of all things and count them as rubbish, in order that I may gain Christ and be found in him, not having a righteousness of my own that comes from the law, but that which comes through faith in Christ, the righteousness from God that depends on faith (Philippians 3:7–9, ESV).

The most difficult lesson to learn and remember in the spiritual life is that we can't save ourselves; in fact, we're hopelessly lost. The Bible tells us in a thousand ways that our only hope of salvation is found in God's plan and through Christ's death. Whether we think of our sins as a debt we owe, a failure to measure up, or an offense to God, the truth is, we're stuck. We can't settle our account, we can't catch up where we've fallen short, and we can't remedy an offense against God on our own. The gospel message is that Christ does all these things for us—if we will let Him. Everything has been arranged, but we have to accept the arrangement. We can't take credit for anything in the salvation God gives us freely in Jesus Christ through faith in Him.

The Apostle Paul was very religious at one time. He wore the official jersey and knew all the spiritual stats. He thought he was a player on God's team but finally realized he had it all wrong. He was trying to use the rules and the law to prove his righteousness and worthiness to God; that is, until God got through to him that he didn't have to try that hard, and that it wouldn't work anyway. Being right with God is all about faith in Christ. Paul had to learn that whatever his role on the team and whatever position he played wasn't what put him on the team; he was there only by God's grace.

In the movie *When The Game Stands Tall*, Arturo turns out to be a hero in one game. He's usually a bench-warmer, but he contributes. He brings an attitude to the team that is crucial to his teammates, even though his skill level is third string. The humility Arturo describes and displays in saying that his real joy is being on the team and with the team is a heartwarming illustration of what grace feels like. It is also a good way to express gratitude to God for saving us and putting us on His team. If we're smart, we'll never assume that our skills are essential and that God couldn't get along without us. At the football level, it's about having a relationship with the rest of the team. At the eternal level that Paul was writing about, it's all about knowing Christ Jesus our Lord.

How do you know you're on God's team?

REFLECTING

GENUINE LOVE

*By the time I came to DLS, I'd moved eleven times.
"That's military life," my mom always said at lights
out. It hurt less not to make friends. These last four
years . . . I found the only friends I've ever had. I'll
never be able to give to you guys all you've given to
me. Best I can do is step up tomorrow and be what a
quarterback should be—a leader.*

—MANNY GONZALES
From the movie *WHEN THE GAME STANDS TALL*

Don't just pretend to love others. Really love them.
Hate what is wrong. Hold tightly to what is good. Love
each other with genuine affection, and take delight
in honoring each other. Never be lazy, but work hard
and serve the Lord enthusiastically. Rejoice in our
confident hope. Be patient in trouble, and keep on
praying (Romans 12:9–12, NLT).

The Bible often repeats itself. This is clearly not because
God forgets what He has said or is not paying attention. He
repeats Himself frequently because *we* don't get the point.
Sometimes we ignore what He says or reject His words
or accept the message without doing anything about His
instructions. So, He patiently repeats Himself . . . again.
Everyone has heard Mom or Dad utter the following words
with a parental tone: "Now, don't make me say this again!" We
should have listened the first time, but God demonstrates His

love for us in that while we often don't listen, He is willing to tell us again.

Today's passage begins by confronting one of our main problems when it comes to loving others. We fake it. Busted! We pretend and put on a nice face when we're seething inside. God knows this, but He doesn't just tell us not to pretend. Stopping a bad behavior is not enough. He says, "Really love them." And then just a little later, so we have a good chance to let it sink in, "Love each other with genuine affection."

Because love is such a big deal in life, God has put stuff about it throughout the Bible. We can't grasp all of love at any time, but we can keep learning and understanding it better as we experience it. For example, the phrase "love each other with genuine affection" has to do with honestly expressing feelings for each other. People we love shouldn't be in doubt about whether we love them or not. Saying, "I love you" may be awkward, but it needs to be said in some way. Guys often get kidded for the clumsy way we put things into words. "I love you, man" is probably as often a punch line in a joke as it is a moment of real connection. But the connection needs to be made.

The team meetings before games with De LaSalle players often include these expressions of genuine affection. Players aren't required to speak, but they know they are in a setting where it's all right to try to put what they feel for the rest of their teammates into words. The quote from Manny Gonzales is a great example. When the expression is genuine, it comes across that way, even if the words are clumsy. That's okay. Love also has a clumsy side.

How can you express your feelings to those you love?

FACING YOUR GIANTS

First time I watched Poly film and saw Buster—I was scared. Then I remembered something Coach Lad told us on my first day of practice: "Face your fears." When I got home that night I pasted Buster's name and number on the ceiling above my bed. Every night since, no matter how tired, I've been saying "Buster Mathews, #99 . . . You. Are. Mine." A hundred times every night. I promise you, we're not gonna lose because of Buster Mathews.

—BEASER
From the movie *WHEN THE GAME STANDS TALL*

The Lord said to Gideon, "With the three hundred men that lapped I will save you and give the Midianites into your hands. Let all the others go home" (Judges 7:7, NIV).

Three hundred men sounds like a nice-sized band of brothers to take into a fight—until you remember that they were going up against an army of 120,000 men. "Outnumbered" doesn't quite describe the difference between the two armies. The story of Gideon is one of the great accounts of not only what a small group of highly motivated and committed people can accomplish, but also what God can do when people recognize that He *always* tips the balance in His favor no matter what the odds.

In the first part of the story, Gideon wanted no part in going up against the Midianites. He was minding his own business, trying to get by without getting in trouble. But God found him and told him he would lead Israel to a great victory against their oppressors. Gideon couldn't see it and was afraid to consider it. He had seen the Midianite game films and didn't think the Israel team had a snowflake's chance in hell of winning. God had to convince Gideon to get a team on the field and the Lord would take care of the outcome. It took some doing on God's part.

Then, when Gideon got a team together of 32,000 men, he surely thought, *Thirty-two thou against a hundred and twenty thou . . . maybe we've got a chance.* But God told him the group was way too large. God wasn't interested in a team that thought it could win; God wanted a team who stepped on the field convinced that win or lose, they were there for God. As a result, only three hundred made the cut.

This story can be found in chapters 6–8 of the book of Judges. The account of the actual attack sounds like a modern-day Special Forces operation. Under the cover of darkness, Gideon's men pulled off a pyrotechnic display that so confused the sleepy Midianites that they ended up turning on each other. Many of the Midianites who died that night were killed by friendly fire. The victory was one for the ages—a tribute to what God can do with a few good men.

In the movie *When The Game Stands Tall*, Beaser, the big lineman, is clearly one of the good guys. Even-tempered, strong, uncomplicated, and a straight thinker, he would have made Gideon's three hundred. His statement about facing his overwhelming opponent was, "I promise you, we're not gonna lose because of Buster Mathews." He knew what he could do, but he didn't assume he could do *everything*. Like Beaser and Gideon, we are challenged to do our part and leave the question of ultimate victory in God's hands.

What challenges are you facing that you have taped to your ceiling?

PERSONAL GOALS

My old man's insane. My mom used to keep him in line, but he wore her out. Once I made the team, I thought he'd be better. . . . But he became an animal. And I hated him. The funny thing is, what saved me was this team. I used to play as hard as I could, thinking that would make him happy. And then I'd be happy. I'm not running for him anymore. I'm running for you. You guys love me whether I'm scoring touchdowns or not. I was missing that, and you guys gave it to me. I don't know how I can ever repay that. . . . Tomorrow I don't play for him, I play for you.

—CHRIS
From the movie *WHEN THE GAME STANDS TALL*

The greatest among you will be your servant. For those who exalt themselves will be humbled, and those who humble themselves will be exalted (Matthew 23:11–12, NIV).

When we read Jesus' teachings, we can think they make sense but then blatantly ignore those teachings when we get on with life. We can imagine, for example, that serving people is a way to greatness, but we don't usually live as though that were true. Instead, we claw our way to the top, stepping on others along the climb. We can act as though greatness means "everybody else serving me."

Towards the end of the movie *When The Game Stands Tall*, Chris, his dad, and Coach Lad run into each other at the store. By this time, we're all a little tired of seeing the dad make a spectacle of himself, riding on his son's achievements as if they were his own. Seldom confrontational with parents, Coach Lad says, "Did Chris show you the thesis he wrote for my class on Matthew 23:12? Amazingly insightful for someone his age. Really terrific. You should read it."

When Mickey asks his son what the verse says, the dad ignores Jesus' point completely and zeros in on the word *exalts*. All he can think about is how much Chris's record will exalt his son and, by extension, him. Chris realizes, however, that his father is not happy and he can't do anything to make his father happy—no matter how many records he breaks or how hard he runs. Going for the record isn't about Chris; it's about his father's internal struggles. His father, trying so hard and so angrily to reach exaltation, is about to be humbled. His son, who is willing to be humble, will end up being exalted.

The statement Jesus made about greatness parallels the statement He made about exaltation. If we want to understand humility, we can start by serving others. Chris realized that he couldn't run for his father because that didn't help, but he *could* run for his teammates because they loved him whether he was scoring touchdowns or not. He discovered the joy of serving his teammates by running as hard as he could. In that service and humility, he arrived at greatness. Putting Jesus' words into practice always takes us a lot further than just agreeing with Him.

In what areas do you need a fresh dose of humility? What will that look like?

COACH ECHO

Your ears shall hear a word behind you, saying,
"This is the way, walk in it," whenever you turn
to the right hand or whenever you turn to the left
(Isaiah 30:21, NKJV).

Isaiah's words about God can be illustrated in a small way by how an effective coach influences his players far beyond the game. When great coaches die, their older players often say they have lived their entire lives still listening to their coach's voice tracking them and saying the same thing Isaiah recorded: "This is the way, walk in it." They may have left that coach far behind physically, but they can still hear his way of approaching situations and making decisions about going left or right. A good coach leaves a lasting echo in your life.

The game stands tall when what we learn on and around the field touches all of life. The rest is just fun. Win or lose the game, it is still a game, but what we take away from the experience is the lasting value that can transform our lives.

Interestingly, the most difficult times to really hear God are when everything is going great *and* everything is falling apart. On regular days, we are more likely to include some attention to God, but real good times and very hard times both tend to drown out His voice. In good times, we get wrapped up in enjoying stuff and don't have time for God; when we're wiped out, we get a little angry or resentful at Him and don't *want* to listen. An extended good time, like an incredible winning streak, has a way of driving this point home because our attention gets shifted to the record and forgets the moment-by-moment choices it took to develop.

We need to remember that a constant in any situation is God speaking. Life is about continuous choices. God allows them to come at us, and He gives us input through His Word. That's part of the reason we can say God is always talking. Just open your Bible and you'll hear God. Sometimes God has definite instructions. As Isaiah puts it, God can tell you to go left or right. Other times, it's your choice. But all the time, God wants to be involved.

When The Game Stands Tall movie ends by tying up some loose ends. The tragedies that happened to Cam with the loss of his mother and his best friend T.K. are left hanging when Cam goes off to Oregon to play college football, but he returns to see De LaSalle's championship game the year The Streak ended. As he watches his former team honor Coach Lad, he realizes that God does have a way of working things out in the long run.

In the moment, events may not make sense. If we keep moving and keep trusting God, however, we will eventually understand His purposes better. We may not like what's happening in our lives at any given moment, but we can always be sure that God is saying, like a great coach, "This is the way, walk in it."

What can you do to hear and experience God's Word daily?